# RHYMES & RECOLLECTIONS OF
# A LAKELAND LAD

by

LEN  HAYTON

Published by Leonard and Jean Hayton



ISBN 978-0-9570942-1-5



Printed by Titus Wilson, Kendal
2016

# CONTENTS



## SECTIONS
## 1. GROWING UP IN LAKELAND



## 2. COURTING & ROMANCE



## 3. A COUNTRY LAWYER'S TALES

# INDEX OF FIRST LINES OF VERSES

In 2005 LH & Joy produced a CD on which they recited a selection of LH's poems. 1500 CDs were sold & the money raised went to local charities as recorded in the Westmorland Gazette.

# FOREWORD

Len has kindly asked me to write this foreword.

He and I met through Guardian Soulmates on the internet in March 2010. Len's former wife, Joy, had sadly died in 2007 and I was single. Little did we think when we first met that our lives would lead to a whirlwind romance and our marriage within four months. My professional background was first in teaching and then in nursing. I always loved the study of literature and my hobbies were in music, as in choral singing, and I was lucky to enjoy travelling in this country and abroad during my holidays.

I have found Len's family and friends and the people of Levens to be delightful, and I am grateful to them for their warm welcome and support. Len's niece informed me that "life with Uncle Len would never be dull." And that is just as I have found it to be! The 18 months since we met have been the happiest time of my life and full of fun and interest. It is amazing what opportunities life can hold in store. I never imagined that one day I would become a pillion passenger on Len's motorbike! Nor did I ever envisage helping my husband to publish a book! Len and I feel very fortunate to have met in the autumn of our lives and to share our appreciation of living in this beautiful part of the world, the English Lake District.

Very soon in our relationship I realised what a man of many interests and talents Len is, and I discovered a treasure trove of his writings. He has written poems and stories for friends and for his own amusement for many years, and his themes cover a wide range of subject matter. For me, hearing his lovely warm Westmorland accent reading his own verses, and other poets' verses that he loves, has been a great joy. One of Len's poems, "After a Ceilidh on

Islay", is hilarious and has everybody in tucks of laughter when he recites it with a Scottish accent! A friend recorded Len reading the poem and now it can be seen on YouTube.

I find Len's writings amusing, informative and often profound as well as poetic. He has a great compassion for humanity and wildlife and this is expressed in his writings as a deep concern for the people of our local community, the natural world and the state of our own beloved nation.

Len's roots are the small hill farm in the Kentmere Valley in the South Lakes where he was brought up, but his profession took him out of this "Shangri-La" and led him into the wider world as a Lakeland lawyer in many varied areas of work, both country-wide and abroad, earning him the Outstanding Achievement Award at the Cumbria Business Awards in 2007.

Len loves the local dialect which he heard and spoke as a boy, and he is enthusiastic in his support of the Lakeland Dialect Society and its intention to keep the various forms of Cumbrian dialect alive. He wants to encourage others to enjoy the character, lovely lilt and humour of its colourful vocabulary and turns of phrase.

This book is a patchwork of Len's life and interests including many of the verses, stories and songs that he has written. He has been well-known in South Cumbria for his entertaining after-dinner speeches and talks on various other occasions, although he is now enjoying a rest from those activities.

I have encouraged Len to publish this book so that people who have heard him speak either in person or on his CD, *'Tales of a Lakeland Lad'*, can now enjoy his verses and stories in print. I hope that many readers, who do not know Len, will enjoy dipping into his writings and receive as much pleasure as I have.

Jean Hayton<br>
5th October, 2011

# ADDENDUM

At the time of writing it is six and a half years since Len and I met and just six years since we married. This time has been the happiest period of my life. Because of Len's positive attitude and unfailing interest in the world about us, we have enjoyed so many experiences together, including our travels in England and the Isle of Man, Scotland and the isles of Islay, Arran and Gigha, Wales, County Donegal in Eire and County Antrim and Rathlin Island in N. Ireland. We honeymooned in California and with Ingrid and family in South Dakota, U.S.A. Most memorably, we holidayed in the area of Interlaken in the Bernese Oberland in Switzerland, a country I had never been to before and which surpassed all expectations with its spectacular natural beauty. More recently we have delighted in our small caravan adventures in the beautiful counties of Dumfries and Galloway and Yorkshire.

In 2014 Len was invited by Hal and Susie Bagot at Levens Hall to be interviewed, purely as a lover of the beautiful gardens there, for a BBC television programme called *Glorious Gardens from Above*. The presenter was the renowned gardening expert Christine Walkden. It was a lovely sunny September day and Len was dressed in his shirt sleeves and red braces. She and Len sat side by side on a wooden bench on the lawn and she roared with laughter when Len described how we had met through the *Guardian Soulmates* website and we had a 91 per cent correlation then, but that now it must 100 per cent, as I was a vegetarian when we first met, but I am not so any longer.

It was great fun for me being involved in the publication of Len's first book *The Collected Tales of a Lakeland Lad* which was a runner-up in the *Cumbria Book of the Year* in 2012. Now I am very much enjoying working with Len on the present revised and abridged version called *Rhymes and Recollections of a Lakeland Lad*. It is taxing both our brains and, as Len always says, it is 'good diversion therapy'!

Over the last twelve months our activities have been restricted by Len's health problems. Nevertheless Len has recovered from some incredibly serious situations and we have lived each day to the full, enjoying the company of family and friends and some lovely meals at nearby Levens Hall, for instance.

I am grateful to all the doctors and nurses, our wonderful family and friends both in the UK and the US, the kind people of our village of Levens, the community of St John's Church in Levens and our vicar, the Rev. Canon Ruth Crossley, for all the tremendous support they have given to both Len and me, particularly over the last twelve months. Thank you from the bottom of my heart.

Jean Hayton,
22nd August, 2016

# INTRODUCTION & CHARITY APPEAL

**Background**

Like many families I have lost close relatives and friends to cancer, including my late wife Joy at Christmas 2007, my brother Jack in 1967 and my brother Gerard in July 2007, my friend and law partner Michael Winkley in January 2010, and my eldest daughter Jacqueline in April 2016. I myself am in the last stages of multiple myeloma.

By the magic of the internet I met Jean in 2010 and we were married in July the same year. It has been a delightfully successful marriage. Jean has been aware of my condition since the beginning.

**Cancer Charity Appeal**

The purpose of this book is to raise £5,000 for Cancer Care South Lakeland and £5,000 for the Hospice at Home based at St John's Hospice in Lancaster, who both care for people affected by cancer in South Lakeland. These charities have provided care and support to my late daughter Jacqueline and her husband Gordon and their two young daughters, as well as myself.

Jean and I have decided to fund the printing and publication of the new book ourselves as our contribution and give all the proceeds to be divided between the above two charities. We intend to print 1000 books and sell them at £10 each, making a total of £5000 to each of the two charities.

Where the books are sold through shops, the retail price will be more to allow for the retailer's commission and raise £10 clear per copy.

★   ★   ★

In 2011 my wife Jean and I published *The Collected Tales of a Lakeland Lad* which ran to 506 pages. It was semi-autobiographical because my journey through life linked my verses and stories and interests together. The book also contained Westmorland and family photos plus snippets of local history. The inspiration and encouragement came from Jean as I acknowledged then and I do now:

*To my Wife and Editor Jean*

*When you read fifty years of my jottings*
*Then collected them all in a pile*
*When you had seen my attempts to write a book*
*You beamed with your wonderful smile.*

*"We're too old to create our own family*
*But I've got an idea," you said*
*"We'll collate all your verses and stories*
*And make a lovely big book instead!"*

Our book proved popular and the print run of 1060 sold out quickly. We have had many requests for a reprint. Our book was intended to be a celebration of life, mainly for family and friends. It was a book just to browse or dip into as the fancy took

We have decided not to reprint the book as a whole but instead to include a selection of material from *The Collected Tales of a Lakeland Lad* in a smaller and lighter publication called *Rhymes & Recollections of a Lakeland Lad*. I have also added some new material. As before, I have included my favourite Lakeland dialect poem, *It's Nobbut Me* by John Richardson, published in 1886.

*Rhymes & Recollections of a Lakeland Lad* is not all written in dialect, but mostly in plain English. Where dialect verses are included, a glossary is available. *To help keep our inheritance of dialect words alive, please have a go at reading the words aloud a few times. It can be fun!*

In the main glossary at the back of the book you can find some of the Norse origins of the words used in this book. If you study place names in Lakeland, you will soon realise how many are devolved from the Norse and Anglian settlements in this part of the world. Small wonder that my ancestors, who all lived in Westmorland, used words which a Norwegian or Icelandic visitor would have easily understood.

We hope you will enjoy the variety of my 'musings and amusings'.

# ACKNOWLEDGEMENTS

It is a pleasure to express our thanks to the people who have been so helpful in the preparation of this book. We thank our family and all the Chums and friends who have encouraged and supported us, especially during the last twelve months.

I am grateful to our good friend Christine Denmead, who has created most of the illustrations. She has succeeded in catching the spirit of Willie the satisfied farmer, as well as the alcoholic lady, the burglar, the joyful display by the tiny birds in *Dew Bath on a May Morning*, the bank voles and the hovering kestrel, and the humour of *This Thing We All Need* and the *Toast to the Hotel and Caterers*.

Special thanks go to my niece Annabel Williams for the wedding photos and the Penny Farthing pictures.

I wish to thank Tommy Coulthard for allowing me to include his lovely dialect poem *The Dawn Chorus* with the illustration in colour by Robbie Ellis. I wish to thank Jean Scott-Smith and all the members of the Lakeland Dialect Society for many years of enjoyment and support.

For all their help and work in the production of this book our grateful thanks go to Bryan Harper for the typesetting and plate preparation, to Steve Edwards for all the costings and admin and proprietor David Rigg and the printing and binding team at Titus Wilson. It has been a pleasure to work with such skilled and helpful people.

# KENTMERE: THE LAKELAND VALLEY WHERE I GREW UP

Kentmere is an idyllic and peaceful valley community which lies nine miles north of Kendal in the south east of the Lake District. The valley has remained largely unspoiled because it lies off the main tourist route with only one access road by car.

Like the sheep which are heafed or hefted to a particular part of a Lakeland fell and nurtured there, my family has lived in Kentmere almost continuously since 1844. My great great grandfather, the Reverend Gerard Hayton, came as curate to Kentmere in 1844 and in 1851 he purchased Brow Top Farm. The farm has been the family home ever since. I was born at Brow Top and brought up there and I lived in Kentmere for fifty years. My male line ancestors lived in the Westmorland parishes of Kentmere, Grayrigg, Orton and Asby from before 1660 and my mother's ancestors came from Levens in Westmorland, where I now live.

The Kentmere valley is margined by a range of beautiful fells and crags sloping into stone-walled enclosures, pastures and meadows on the valley floor. To go through the valley to Troutbeck in the west, Haweswater in the north or Longsleddale in the east, one must walk over Garburn, Nan Bield or Stile End passes respectively. These passes were in times past pack-horse tracks and communication routes before turnpike roads were constructed from Kendal to Appleby and Ambleside in 1762. The houses and farms scattered about the valley are built of stone and slate in the traditional Lakeland style. One can often find a spring as the source of water and a small quarry near at hand, where the stone for the dwelling has been hewn from the rock.

An old Roman road from Galava camp at Ambleside to Brougham follows a route over the range of fells behind the summits of Yoke, Ill Bell and Froswick and crosses High Street above the head of the valley basin. In the 1870s my great-grandfather, Richard Mattinson, a gamekeeper on Kentmere Hall Estate, used to collect dotterel feathers on High Street to make his flies for fishing. He fished from a boat on "Kentmere Broadwater", now known as Kentmere Tarn.

It seems odd to us now that sporting occasions, including traditional wrestling and horse racing and shepherds' meets, were held so high in the fells on High Street. However, when we look at the topography we see that High Street is mainly level on the top and is a central meeting point for the people of the valleys of Kentmere, Longsleddale, Mardale, Martindale and Patterdale with access to Hartsop and Howtown. Lakeland folk were used to walking fair distances to country dances and merry neets in those days! Frank Garnett in *Westmorland Agriculture 1800-1900* tells us that the last shepherds' meet (a meeting to exchange stray sheep) was held on High Street fell in 1835.

Kentmere Dale Head in winter by Geoffrey Berry

In recent years the Kentmere Horseshoe, which includes High Street, has become a favourite circuit for fell-walkers and fell-runners. The annual fell race has generated more interest in Kentmere and increased the number of visitors. Walkers and cyclists as well as bird watchers, wildlife enthusiasts and local history buffs can all find something of interest in Kentmere.

It is thrilling to watch a pair of majestic golden eagles, easily identified by the length of their wings and primaries, circling high above Kentmere or see a peregrine falcon dive at wondrous speed out of the sky. Equally, to sit at peace with binoculars near the re-made Kentmere Tarn or the plantation and observe the wonders of nature around you is a joy in itself.

When I was born at Brow Top Farm in 1940, the houses and land in the valley were mainly occupied by farmers and their workers. In addition there were quarrymen working at the quarries in Dale Head and workers extracting diatomite from the site of the old Kentmere Tarn.

The Kentmere form of Lakeland dialect was spoken by my parents, grandparents and neighbours. Hopefully, the verses and stories which follow give a flavour of the period.

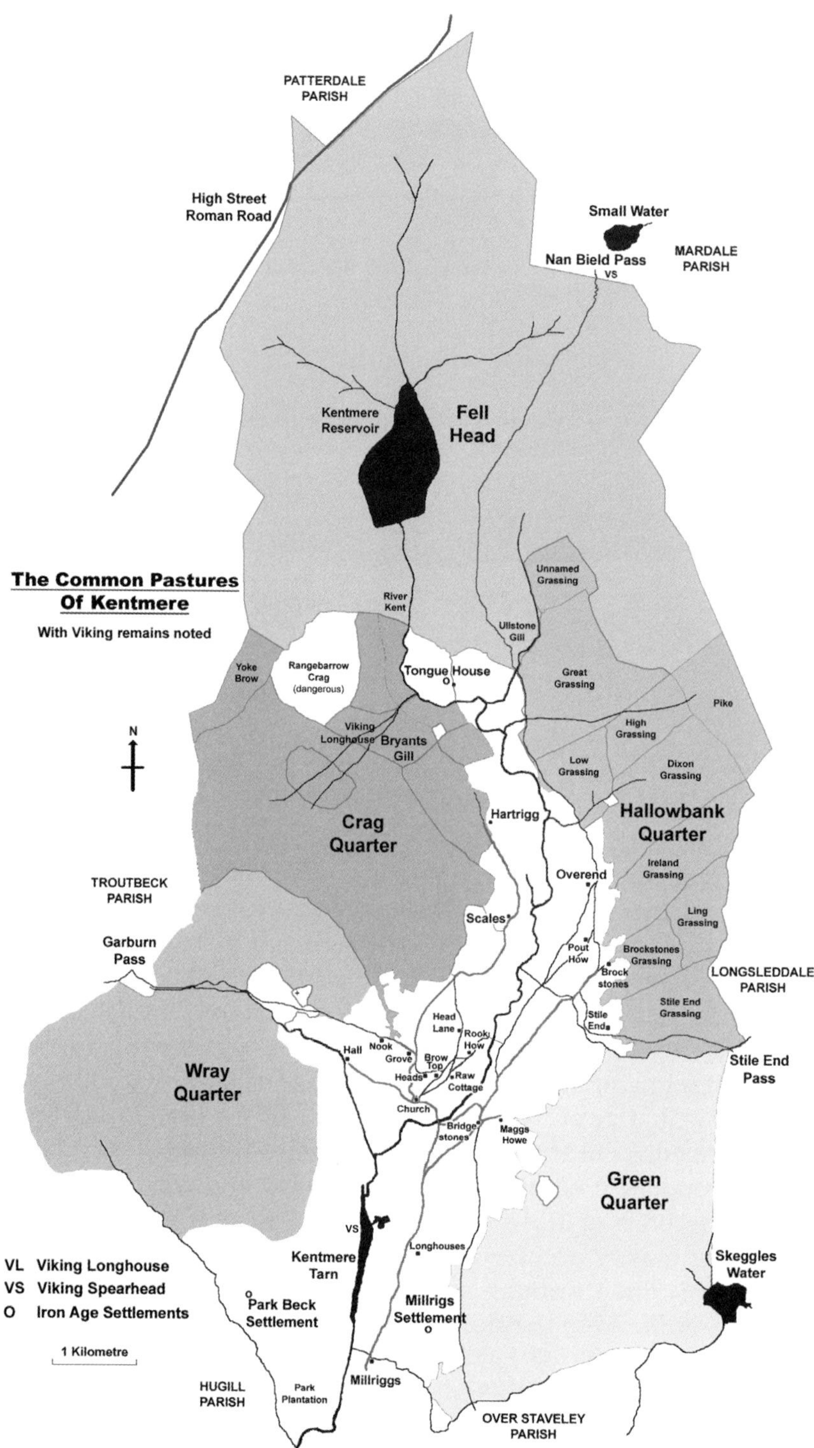


The Robert Ridley Plan shows the Common Pastures on which Robert has kindly added the locations of Bryants Gill longhouse and Viking finds in Kentmere.

## *1*

# GROWING UP IN LAKELAND

## GROWING UP ON A LAKELAND HILL FARM
### Brow Top in Kentmere

I was born in April 1940, a month before Winston Churchill took over the conduct of the Second World War from Neville Chamberlain.

For me the year 1945 recalls picking "spuds" (potatoes) with our land girl, Eva Kinchin, in Cross Howe, a fertile field which the War Ag had requisitioned my father to plough.

Picture shows us picking potatoes in Kentmere. Left to right: Father, L.H., landgirl Eva Kinchin and brother Gerard. Mother took the picture with a box Brownie camera.

At that time Brow Top was the home of my parents, Evelyn Mary Hayton and Joseph Hayton, my two brothers Gerard and Jack and me, plus our paternal Granny, our land girl Eva, a farm man and a maid. The farm produced sufficient to sustain us and also produced butter from fourteen pedigree dairy Shorthorns. We had a butter round and Father delivered the butter each Saturday in an old Singer van to our customers in Staveley, Burneside and Kendal.

We had a flock of Rough Fell sheep as well as hens, ducks and turkeys – all wandering around our typical small Lakeland mixed farm.

# FREE RANGE
## True Freedom!

**Glossary**

| | | |
|---|---|---|
| **Aboot** = about | **Inta** = into | **Oppen'd** = opened |
| **Be-ad** = bed | **Ivvery** = every | **Pig-hull** = pigsty |
| **Cem** = came | **Laik** = play | **Roond** = round |
| **Commen** = coming | **Lile** = little | **Se-an** = soon |
| **Dew** = do | **Mornen** = morning | **Ta** = to |
| **En** = and | **Naybody** = nobody | **Ut** = at |
| **Fer** = for | **Neet** = night | **War** = were |
| **Fre** = for | **Nin** = none | **Wi'** = with |
| **Gat** = got | **O'** = of | **Wud** = would |
| **Git** = get | **Oor** = our | **Wus** = was |

My education started
Like many lile lads fre Lakeland
Growen up on a bonny dale farm
I'd freedom ta run en ta laik aboot
En naybody wud dew us harm.

Oor parents gat up se-an ivvery mornen
Thur wus nin o' this liggen in be-ad
We'd ta lowp up en git t'day started
Wi' drive en ideas in yer he-ad!

We kept oor poultry locked up ut neet
Fer fear o' t' fox commen by
But when we oppen'd up in t' mornen
Eager inta free air
All t' hens wud fly.

Turkeys growen plump fer Christmas
Crowded gobblen through t' door
While ducks en geese cem waddlen
Quacken, hissen, chatteren,
Numbered by t' score.

On t' in-bye pastures roond oor farm
Rough Fell sheep war grazen
En poultry wander'd far en wide
Gatheren grubs en morsels,
In variety quite amazing!

T' pig was in his pig-hull
T' horse wus eaten hay
Wi' kindness en co-operation
We hed free range ivvery day!

LH: 6.8.2016

LH with Rough Fell pet lamb on
wall at Brow Top – July 1949

In addition Mother did bed and breakfast and we had regulars who came year after year. Mum was a wonderful cook. Her casseroles and red currant and raspberry pasties were delectable – sadly the visitors never left any over!

Outside was the male domain but the "womenfolk" expected the same standards of cleanliness and order outside that applied inside the house. There was no toilet in the house until 1952. The closet, "thunderbox" or "t'lile hoose" (dry soil toilet) was up the yard. It was a solid stone and slated lean-to on the end of the old barn or hoghus (animal shed in old Norse). The hoghus was then used as a workshop and store. There was a lovely view across the valley from the open door of the closet as the sun rose over Green Quarter fell.

Our closet had a long wooden seat with a large hole for Father and Mother to use and a small one for me. I would sometimes join one of my parents at the closet where we chatted and I learned about the basics of life from them. Later I likened the debates we had there to consultations with the Oracle at Delphi! They call it "bonding" nowadays.

The closet was my first "college", for I'm sure the bonding of love and respect for my parents and the sound basis of life they gave me had its origin there.

It was cleaned out from below each spring through a "hog-hool" (hole) which was behind a large stone slab leaning against the wall. The south-west wind whistled through the gap between the slab and the wall and acted as a giant extractor fan. There was no necessity for air fresheners and no time was wasted on the closet in cold weather!

LH's grandparents Gerard Albert Hayton and Mary Lib with my mother Evelyn and brothers Gerard and Jack. *c.*1935

Father mowing banking with a ley (lja ON for a scythe)

Eva, our landgirl, and my mother Evelyn with farm dog

The kitchen fire rarely went out in winter. Each morning my mother would rake the ashes, set the kindling and stir the fire to life before her first visit to the closet. Nothing was wasted, not even the daily paper – toilet rolls were a luxury. Food scraps went to the pig and in due course we ate the pig! There was no need to segregate waste – it was used or re-cycled through the pig or the closet!

I remember Mother getting agitated in the morning if the kindling was damp! Her closet routine was sometimes delayed when the fire wouldn't light. She needed the "black nanny" (kettle) to be ready boiling when she returned from the closet and the fire ready to cook the porridge.

You see time could not be wasted on the toilet. *"Ye hed ta lowse doon garn tul t'closet and fasten up yer gallases (braces) as ye cem away."* Today we take for granted a warm bathroom and toilet. It was different then with the wind howling up the valley. Going to the toilet up the yard last thing at night and first thing in the morning was a bracing experience.

# T' KENT'MER COLLEGE

My education started
On the day that I was born
In oor white-weshed Kent'mer farmhouse
On a bonny April morn.

I can't remember howling
Or t'hippins oot to dry
But I do recall correction
At the hint of any lie.

"Speak nobbut truth mi lad," they said
"Cost it what it will
He that hides the wrang he dew-eth
Doth the wrang thing still."

These words cem doon fre t'elders
Etched upon mi varra soo-al
As Dad and I sat side by side
Upon the closet hoo-al.

Oor se-at of early larnin
Was oor closet in the dale
Which had stood through many centuries
Withstanding ivvery gale.

T'se-at was smooth en polished
With countless years of wear
And we didn't need de-odorants
In oor healthy Kent'mer air.

The wood was warm as we sat doon
Cald plastic yet unknown
Nor were we interrupted
By t'discord of t'mobile phone.

There was allus a gurt hoo-al fer Father
And allus a lile hoo-al fer me
We sat side by side on the closet
As he passed on his wisdom to me.

Mainly-what we'd hev doo-er opp-en
As t'sun com up o'er t'hill
"Git thisel up in a morning Lad":
I can remember mi first lesson still!

# FREEDOM UNDER LAKELAND'S DOME OF SKY

## Reflections on growing up in Kentmere

Like many born in the countryside I used to lie on my back on a beautiful day in a meadow and smell the grass and wild flowers or sit on a steep fell-side under the dome of a Lakeland sky admiring the birds, flowers and nature all around. It is a simple luxury which costs nothing. I used to sit and look around marvelling at the wonders of creation. All nature seemed in tune, albeit in the raw.

Following a concert in January 1999 held at Levens Hall with Annie Mawson★ singing and playing so beautifully on her Celtic harp, I wrote this song for her the following morning. It recalls my feelings as a boy and as a man lying on the grass in Kentmere among the fells of Lakeland with the dome of the sky above me. Annie sang it the following year at her Millennium concert in Levens Hall.

### UNDER LAKELAND'S DOME OF SKY
*(The Millennium Dome in Lakeland)*

O the Lakeland hills are calling
And the bonny mountain streams
This loveliest part of England
Fills all my waking dreams.

*Chorus:*
*Where the Herdwick sheep are grazing*
*And the falcon circles high*
*I am part of Mother Nature*
*Under Lakeland's dome of sky.*

When I walk those fells of Lakeland
Then my worries fly away
And freedom: I can touch it
On a glorious summer's day.

*Chorus*

There are mighty rocks and pinnacles
Which attract the mountaineers
Inspiring youth and aged alike
To explore as though pioneers.

*Chorus*

Our lakes and tarns of Lakeland
Mirror mountains rising high
To the dome of blue up yonder
Where cirrus paints the sky.

*Chorus*

O it's there at the Millennium
I'll awake as comes the dawn
To walk my favourite fells of Lakeland
On a "hasky" winter's morn.

*Chorus:*
*Where the Herdwick sheep are grazing*
*And the falcon circles high*
*I am part of Mother Nature*
*Under Lakeland's dome of sky.*

*Hasky: A Lakeland dialect word meaning a sharp frosty morning, clear and bright.*

*c.* LH: 20.January 1999; revised 15th January 2000

* Annie Mawson M.B.E. is the founder of and runs the wonderful Sunbeams Music Trust. She creates so much happiness and inspiration for disabled adults and young folk alike with her music therapy. Annie put my verse to music and she plays and sings it on the CD which I published in 2005, *Tales of a Lakeland Lad.* See colour section for picture of Annie singing and playing her harp.

# T' KENT'MER KIDS' HUNT AT KIRK SCHOOL

A fun lunchtime at Kentmere Church of England School circa 1948.
Miss Jessie Braithwaite from Staveley was our long-suffering teacher.

Teacher Miss Jessie Braithwaite and children at Kentmere School

Hev you ivver hard o' yon Kent'mer Kids' Hunt
Yance hunted fre t'school up Kent dale?
We ran through Crag Quarter en up o'er t'Yoke
Then doon o'er t'crags en pas t'Scale.

Oor hunt allus started just efter hey noon
When t'school-missus sent us ta dine
But we'd miss oor dinner en git that bit thinner
Ta ga hunten when t'weather was fine.

Scholars of all ages would join in the chase
Loup woes, scale hedges and hill
Then baying like hoonds,
Would mak all hunten soonds
Like a pack ga'en in fer t'kill.

Well yan sick time, I remember it weel
Lile Ben was t'Fox that day
We'd count up ta fifty, ta give him a start
En mak sure he gat on his way.

Generally what humans don't stink like a fox
En hoonds hev a sensitive nose
We're disadvantaged: we run on two legs
En oor nostrils don't track, I suppose.

Now oor Huntsman that day
Shouted, "Hark hark away!"
Young Ben to the Garburn did steer
Up o'er sheep knotts and Sid Leyland's front lots
Us Hoonds did bark at his rear.

Then doon by t'Scale and across t'mid dale
To Stile End en Green Quarter fell
T'Fox it med out ta Maggs Howe or nowt
En t'chase was beginning to tell.

Ben scrammelled up a gurt wo', too hey and too tall
Like a Swardle that's lost its he-ad
En he dived fre the top, far too late fer ta stop
En sank like a gurt lump of le-ad!

Deep in the dipping tub he fell through green slime
En surfaced gasping wi fright
Us Hoonds in the chase were flummoxed by his face
Which was covered with sheep wool and sh… (sheep trunlins!)

We laughed off oor socks at this ill-fated Fox
But stinking he quickly climbed back
Then ta oor surprise wi wild flashing eyes
Our quarry turned on the attack!

Pursued by his stink we hed nay time to think
We fled down the lane back ta school
Ben in a state, Hoonds half an hour late
We were in fer a "touch of the rule".

Jessie walloped us all as we went through the hall
Save the Fox with the terrible pong
Then we suffered that reek fer darn near a week
That sure was fox hunting gone wrong!

LH *c.* 1975

## Glossary

**Allus** = always
**Crag Quarter** = North West Quarter of the Valley. See Index Ref. to Border Tenure & Kentmere Quarters.
**Doon** = down
**Efter** = after
**En** = and
**Fer** = for
**Fre** = from
**Gat** = got
**Garburn** = Garburn Pass, Kentmere to Troutbeck
**Generally what** = usually
**Green Quarter** = South East Quarter of the Valley
**Gurt** = great
**Hard** = heard
**Hev** = have
**Hey** = high
**Hoonds** = hounds
**Ivver** = ever

**Knott** = small, peaked hill
**Loup** = jump
**Mak** = make
**Med** = made
**Nay** = no
**O'** = of
**O'er** = over
**Oor** = our
**Scale** = Scale Farm
**Scrammelled** = scrambled
**Sheep lots** = enclosed sheep fields
**Sick** = such
**Soonds** = sounds
**Swardle** = Swaledale sheep
**Ta** = to
**Trunlins** = sheep droppings or muck
**Wi** = with
**Wo'** = dry-stone field wall
**Woes** = walls
**Yance** = once

# NANCY
## My favourite cow

After Father or my eldest brother Gerard had finished milking, it was my job as a small boy to walk the cows half a mile up the lane from Brow Top through Rook Howe yard to our meadows further up the valley before going to school. The cows would only walk at their own speed. Old Tom, my collie dog, kept them in line when need be. Tom was intelligent and loyal. He was my best pal and companion as I grew up in the valley.

LH with his intelligent dog, Tom.

It was all a very relaxed pace and procedure. I had time to watch the birds and marvel at the spring flowers, look for tadpoles in the boggy ground behind the water-hole while the cows stopped for a drink. Then I would open the gate for them to walk past the footbridge and along to the meadows.

Nancy, my favourite cow, usually walked along chewing her cud towards the rear of the herd. I would lean against her and pull her in to the lane-side and stop close by the wall. There was an ideal mounting block which enabled me to climb on her back. Then she would amble on in a leisurely fashion, seemingly unconscious of my seated presence. She was a docile and kindly animal and she holds a special place in my childhood memories.

My parents farmed a small hill farm
Near the Church up Kentmere Dale
And Mother churned on Thursdays
To fill butter kits for sale.

The butter was so tasty
It was always in demand
Dad said, "It comes fre t'Shorthorns
It's the finest in the land."

My favourite cow was Nancy
When I was just a boy
She was quiet, cuddly and tender
And always rather coy.

We walked in step each morning
So far along the lane
Her thighs she wiggled as she walked
She felt warm in wind and rain.

Her skin was soft like velvet
Underneath her lovely chin
And often when I stroked it
I'm sure I saw her grin!

I rode on her back some mornings
And sometimes home at night
Her back felt smooth like a camel
So it was hard to sit her right.

She plodded home beneath me
But her belly was so wide
I did the splits upon her
I could hardly sit astride.

Her spine was hard and notchy
Her hide as soft as silk
Her "bag" four-square beneath her
Was bulging full of milk.

Unlike a horse she held her head
More closely to the ground
Precarious it was to say the least
No cow's saddle to be found!

Nancy was a pedigree Shorthorn
I wish you could see her now
I trained her to act as my pony
For she was an intelligent cow!

# GARN A' BULLIN

### Taking Nancy to be serviced by the bull

**Glossary**

**Garn a' bullin** = going with or taking a cow to the bull when it is on heat
**Gay happy** = quite happy
**Kytle** = a smock or loose jacket worn by farmers
**Yam** = home

Each year the cows were put to the bull when they "cem a bullin". It was not economic for smaller farms in the valley to keep a bull all year round just to service fourteen cows – as in our case. So it was that my first sight of real sexual intercourse occurred when Father asked me to help him walk Nancy to Millriggs Farm. I would be six or seven years old.

Millriggs was a large farm, a mile down the valley, where Jim Iceton kept a fine bull. Father had an arrangement with him to use his bull to service our cows. That morning Nancy didn't seem herself. She was frisky and unsettled and would have nothing to do with me. Father walked behind Nancy and my job was to run forward, stand at road ends and gateways and keep her heading south. I ran in front but she still tried to pass me. We were soon there and this is my recollection of what occurred.

My face drained white with astonishment
As it rose before my eyes
Like the mighty horn of the unicorn
It pointed to the skies.

I had trotted a mile with Nancy
For she was my favourite cow
She seemed in a hurry to get there
She was eager and frisky somehow.

Then I was six or seven
Grown up in my father's cap
A walking stick higher than I was
"Just William" my favourite chap!

I goggled at this mighty bull
Its thighs like limbs of oak
I held my breath, my eyes were wide
Tension, no one spoke!

Taurus reared in silhouette
Against the morning sky
And I knew in my heart that this was the start
But I had no inkling why.

For you have to see it was new to me
This need for copulation
Naïve lile Len, I didn't know then
How to renew the population.

Nancy quivered as the bull rose high
Her legs began to quake
I feared for Nancy and grabbed Dad's arm
I was sure her legs would break.

"Poor Nancy!" I cried and buried my head
Under my father's kytle
He stroked my hair and said "Noo lad
Thou'll find this sort o' thing is vital.

"We need good semen fre a bull
A bull with conformation
With powerful muscles in its legs
To achieve that penetration.

"Well noo lad, just dry thy eyes
Fer Nancy looks quite snappy
Her eyes are bright, her head held high
She'll set off yam gay happy."

That primeval thrust, the spark of lust
Had died away in Taurus
Charmed by the balm of post–coital calm
He joined in the morning chorus.

As we turned for home, I could not have known
How another large bull one day,
Would cause me to study the pedigrees of
The famous Poll Charolais.

The experience with Nancy's courtship was to prove useful. A case which involved some contention between breeders of horned Charolais and hornless Poll Charolais cattle arose in 1984. As a result I became the secretary of a new cattle breed society for five years, which involved a diversion from my ordinary legal work. I had an interesting time travelling to farms in England, Wales, Scotland and Northern Ireland – also to the USA, Canada, Hungary, France and Switzerland.

# BLUEBELL WOOD

Some weekends after I had taken the cows to the meadows in spring and summer, I used to get diverted. I sat either by the river Kent or on the footbridge watching the brown trout and crayfish. Sometimes I saw a white-throated dipper searching for mayflies and caddis larvae.

Just up Low Dote, the rocky field between the river and the lane to Pout Howe, there is a lovely view of the upper valley from near the stile and split rock. *Dote* or *Dalt* was the name given originally to a specified share in an open field. Following the Inclosure Acts 1757 to 1830 for the improvement of agriculture, many of such areas were walled off, as in this case. When I was a lad the Low and High Dotes belonged to my Father.

Sometimes I went across the footbridge, up the path through Low Dote and along the lane to Bluebell Wood on the east side of the River Kent. It was a lovely peaceful place. I felt like St Francis of Assisi with nature all around me. I used to wander down the "lonnin" (lane) under a canopy of hazel trees and into Bluebell Wood which slopes down to the river.

★   ★   ★

# BLUEBELL WOOD

There's a picture in my memory
Of a wonderful woodland glade
Where sunbeams shone through the canopy
In a sprinkling of light and shade.

Before I grew to manhood
I used to wander in the wood
To observe and savour nature
As every human should.

Hazel, silver birch and alder
Seemed to gossip in the breeze
But oak stood firm for England
The Monarch of English trees.

A red squirrel dashed for cover
Song birds sounded the alarm
But my disturbance was soon forgotten
When I lay down in the woodland calm.

I stayed in that dell for hours
In a sea of bluebell blue
While below the bank beneath the brow
The busy beck splashed through.

And from the dappled water
A dipper would appear
Then bob upon a mossy rock
And as quickly disappear.

Where aconites and snowdrops
Had seen late winter snow
When the warmth of vibrant springtime
Made oxlip and primrose glow.

In spring the woodland butterflies
Fluttered in the sun
The brimstone and the orange tip
On their annual nectar run.

While still I lay, the woodland birds
Were busy all around
Wood pigeon, wren and woodpecker
With their distinctive sounds.

The nuthatch and the blue tit
The great tit and the thrush
The blackbird, finch and bunting
Building nests in tree and bush.

But always there was a reason
That I could no longer stay
So I promise and I promise myself
I'll return to that glade one day!

## T'MILKEN

My "Milken Verse" recalls life on our Lakeland family farm in the 1940s and 50s. It was my first attempt at writing in my family's form of Lakeland dialect. *So have a go! Read the verses out loud a few times to savour them and get the feel of the words handed down to us by our forefathers.*

Our landgirl Eva Kinchin milking a cow in the yard at Brow Top.

## Glossary

**Atween** = between
**Ba-eth** = both
**Be-us** = beasts or cows
**Byre** = shippen, shuppen or cow house
**Black nanny** = kettle smoked black over
the fire
**Brat** = course apron
**Coo band** = rope neck collar for tying up a
cow
**Coppy** = three legged stool
**Coves** = calves
**Cravacked** = stiff backed
**Gallasses** = braces – suspenders
**Gang** = feeding passage or gangway
between two rows of skell-boose
**Gay** = rather
**Gloo-ered** = looked around hard to see
**Greap or gripe** = channel where dung and
urine dropped.
**Guss** = grass
**Gussins** = grassings or pastures
**Hurpl-en** = limping, stiff with age
**Kine** = cows
**Laiken** = playing
**Laa groond** = low ground or bottom fields
**Liggen** = lying down
**Lile** = little

**Loosed doon mi gallasses** = unfastened
my braces
**Lowped** = jumped
**Milk be-us** = milk beasts or milk cows
**Milken side** = space between cow and rud-
stake where there is room to sit to milk
**Nobbut** = only
**O** = all
**Pap** = teat
**Poddish** = oat porridge
**Pow** = wooden pole
**Ring widdy** = a ring swivel ring to which
the cow band was attached
**Rough brat** = apron made from sackcloth.
**Rud-stake** = pole in centre of skel-boose
between two cows.
**Sarra t'coves** = feed or serve the calves
**Se-an** = soon
**Settlestean** = bed where cow lies down.
**Shippen or shuppen** = cowhouse or byre
**Skel-boose** = cow stall for a pair of cows
**Sowked en eased ut ivvery pap** =
squeezed and eased milk by hand from
every teat
**Thowt** = thought
**Yan** = one

# T'MILKEN

I gat up gay early
Yan fine summer's morn
Mi he-ad hardly wakken
It was nobbut just dawn.

I lowped oot of bed
And I gloo-ered oot ta see
If o' oor milk be-us
Wer waiten fer me.

There was some craa-ken in t'hen hoose
En t'cockerel he sang
While doon Foxthwaite gussings
T'mornin chorus fair rang.

I thowt it was se-an
Fer tur wakken up t'wife
Cos she helps sarra t'coves
She's a gay busy life.

So I went oot ta t'closet
In t'fresh mornin air
If thoo looks ta t'priorities
Thoo hessen't a care.

I loused doon mi gallasses
En gat on wi mi job
While I whistled fer t'farm dogs
Either Lassie or Bob.

But it was oor auld Tom
That com hurplen aroond
So I whistled en sent him
In t'laa ground.

While Tom brought be-us
Up in t'byre
I went in t'kitchen
En kindled up t'fire.

I picked up t'Black Nanny
And hinged it on t'crane
Then I mixed oor poddish
And went oot again.

O t'coos in each skel–boose
Wer chowen their cud
Divided bi t'rud-stake
A gurt pow o' wood.

I clattered up t'shuppen
Wi mi coppy and pail
And I lowped inta t'gang
O'er t'skel-boose rail.

I gev em some cake
En a lile bit of hay
'Cos they let doon their milk
Far better that way.

At milken side on mi coppy I sat
While I held mi pail atween mi rough brat
I soaked and I cased at ivvery pap
En t'coos stood content while some hed a nap.

Yer can git turble cravacked
Sitten milken a coo
Thur wer nay fangled machines
Sick as farmers hev noo.

But I'll tell o' you fell-as
Who sleep in til nine
Ta git up at five
En then milk o thi kine.

It's better than liggen
En laiken wi wife
Cos it stengthens thi muscles
En calms o thi strife.

En while I'd been milken
Oor hens hed been fed
En t'Missus hed gitten
Oor oat poddish weel med.

Ham en fresh eggs
We ba-eth can enjoy
What! It's allus been t'same
Sen I was a boy.

★   ★   ★

This verse was put to music in the 1970s and is sung by Robbie Ellis on his CD and also later by Craig Duggan on his CD: *Songs of Cumbria.*

I have also been recorded reading *T'Milken* in dialect for visitors to the Museum of Lakeland Country Life at Abbot Hall in Kendal.

# NOBBUT A COUNTRY LAD'S VIEW
## Written for the Lakeland Dialect Service in Kentmere Church

Granny Hayton in the porch at Brow Top.
Mary Elizabeth Hayton (née Mattinson)

**Glossary**

**Aboot** = about
**Afoor** = before
**Boggles** = ghosts
**Boo** = bow
**Bumly** = bumble bee
**Doon** = down
**Flayt** = frightened
**Freet** = fright
**Gurt** = great
**Hoo** = how
**Kirk** = church
**Lang** = long
**Larn** = learn
**Laiked** = played
**Leet** = light

**Likesear** = likewise
**Lile** = little
**Lish** = agile
**Loup** = jump
**Mair** = more
**Marra** = friend
**Mebbe** = maybe
**Mudder** = mother
**Neet** = night
**Nebbers** = neighbours
**Ner** = Nor
**Nobbut** = only
**Noo** = now
**O** = all
**O'** = of

**Oorsels** = ourselves
**Poddish** = porridge
**Reet** = right
**Sarved** = served
**Sae** = so
**Sed** = said
**Sen** = since
**Shud** = should
**Steean** = stone
**Thur's** = there is
**Varra** = very
**Weel** = well
**Wod** = would

When I was lile en nobbut a lad
Mi Mudder sed to me
Git off ta t'kirk wi Granny lad
Larn Christ-ian-ittee.

I larn't aboot ald Moses' Law
En his gurt slabs o' steean
I memorised t'Commandments
While I laiked aboot doon t'lane.

But Jesus seemed ta git it reet
Least sae't seemed ta me
"Just treat thi nebbers nicely like
As thou'd like em ta treat thee."

"Gentle Jesus meek and mild"
Was t'prayer we sed at neet
Then agen afoor t'poddish
In t'mornin at first leet.

Thur's nay need ta be flayt aboot boggles
Ner loup up in t'air wi freet
If thoo tells o thi troubles ta Jesus
En says a lile prayer at neet.

Sen then oor world has altered
En likesear oor country talk
But not oor simple faith in Thee
T'faith o' country folk.

Varra lile wi boo en scrape noo
But mebbe mair we shud
But we sense oor God aroond us
In ivverything that's good.

We praise Jesus for o t'seasons
His sunleet and his rain
Wild roses in oor hedgeraas
En blossoms doon oor lane.

Deep in oorsels we find Jesus
If nobbut we wod see
Hoo his luv is o aboot us
Hoo wondrous it wod be.

In sunbeams on a fell he-ad beck
In the peace of a woodland glade
We can feel the living Jesus
In ivverything he's me-ad.

That feeling of joy in a job weel done
T'skill in a craftman's hands
We can see hoo the love o' Jesus
Has spread through many lands.

When we're thrang as a bumly in Springtime
En as lish as a gurt March hare
When we're riven at life like a beaver
We're nobbut happy when Jesus is theer.

What a Marra we've gitten in Jesus
He was nobbut a country lad
He sarved his time as a joiner
En he loved folk good en bad.

His spirit of life is within us
His love through joy and pain
Hoo great er the blessin's of Jesus
Lang may his teachin's reign.

*c.* LH 19.6.1988

When in later years I read the annual edition of Giles' cartoons at Christmas, his sketch of Grandma Giles always reminded me of "Mary Eliazabeth" – my granny. She took me to Church because I am sure she wanted me to be a parson like my great great grandfather, Reverend Gerard Hayton. He was the parson at Kentmere from 1846 to 1880. I had to blow the organ but sometimes I forgot to blow for the psalms. Then the notes yawned to a stop until I woke up! I got a toffee for blowing the organ but not if I missed blowing on time! It seemed I was not cut out to be a parson!

Grandfather Hayton mowing with horses in High Meadow.

# FATHER RODE A MOTOR BIKE
## Reflections on Global Warming

Father rode a motor bike
Grandad rode a horse
Great-grandad walked a lot
I drive a car of course!

Father used a little oil
Grandad only grease
Great-grandad was fit and strong
I'm overweight and wheeze!

Father bought a motor car
When I was just a boy
Grandad scoffed and said
"Mi lad, it's just a nasty toy."

Grandad died and things were bad
World War Two was on
So Father bought a tractor
To help the war along.

Father started t'Fordson
Did it all by hand
Developed mighty muscles
Working on the land.

Now hydraulics lift the plough
We've air-conditioned cabs
Time to go to barbecues
Eat skewered scorched kebabs!

Father used less fossil fuel
Grandad hardly any
Great-grandad never heard of it
It cost him not a penny.

The world goes on in cycles
As from centuries before
Survival of the fittest
Was always Nature's law.

Generations mark the milestones
Along Man's road endeavour
But have we kept the balance
Or are we just too clever?

For Father rode a motor bike
Grandad rode a horse
Great-grandad he walked a lot
I drive a car, of course!

*c.* LH 29.6.1978

# 2

# COURTING & ROMANCE

## LH: A WAR BABY

It must hev bin se-an on in August
Back in nineteen thirty-nine
Joseph mi Fadder was forty-fower
And Mudder was thurty-nine.

T'hay moo must hev been gay comfy
Sae pleasing en smellen sae sweet
That Fadder persuaded oor Mudder
Ta hev a lile cuddle en treat.

I was telt I was nobbut an efter-thowt
Mi brothers were upwards of ten
When pre-war on t'hay moo up Kentmer
Mi parents created lile Len.

Then Chamberlain lan't back fre Munich
Wid Hitler's promises worth nowt!
Fer it wasn't lang til poor Poland
Fell under his Panzers' clowt.

Lile Len was born se-an on in April
Just afoor Winston took o'er in May
What wid him en t'brave Battle of Britain
We're safe en we're o' here today!

LH 5.11.06

Thank you to those men and women from all nations
who fought for our freedom.

**Glossary**

| | |
|---|---|
| **Afoor** = before | **Lile** = little |
| **Clowt** = clout | **Mudder** = Mother |
| **En** = and | **Nowt** = nothing |
| **Fadder** = Father | **Sae** = so |
| **Fre** = from | **Se-an on** = early on |
| **Hay moo** = haystack in the barn | **Ta** = to |
| **Hev** = have | **Telt** = told |
| **Lan't back** = landed or came back | |

# "IT'S NOBBUT ME!"
### *"It's Only Me."*

This lovely old poem by John Richardson in his book *Cummerland Talk*, published in 1886, is one of my favourite old dialect verses to recite. It is in Cumberland dialect which differs a little from Westmorland in pronunciation and spelling but is a delight to read. The words in the poem are spelled just as Richardson wrote them in his book, but in Kentmere in Westmorland we would tend to say "knaa" instead of "know" and "whaa" instead of "who". The poem is so well known throughout Cumbria that I believe it has been recited in the vernacular dialects of many of our Cumbrian villages and hamlets.

Please read it aloud a few times so that you can enjoy the sound of good old Lakeland speech for yourself.

It recalls the old way of courting in the valleys. Often parents would retire to bed and allow their daughter to wait downstairs for her sweetheart to call. If he was a welcome visitor, she would leave the door latch open. The latch was called the "sneck". To lock the door all one did was to put a wedge above the sneck.

If the would-be suitor was unwelcome, she would "sneck possit him": i.e. put the wedge in the sneck, so as to keep him out.

In this poem the young man was obviously welcome!

# "IT'S NOBBUT ME!"
*A tale of courting in the old days*
*by John Richardson, 1817-1886*

Ya winter neet, I mind it weel
Oor lads hed been t' fell
An' bein' tir't, went seun ta bed,
An' I sat be mysel'.
I hard a jike on t' window pane,
An' deftly went to see;
An' when I ax't, "Who's jiken theer?"
Says t' chap: "It's nobbut me!"

"Who's *me?*" says I, "What want ye here?
Oor fwok er aw i' bed." –
"I dunnet want your fwok at aw
It's *thee* I want," he sed.
"What cant'e want wi' me?" says I;
"An' who, the deuce, can't be?
Just tell me who it is, an' than" –
Says he, "It's nobbut me."

"I want a sweetheart an' I thowt
Thou mebbe wad an' aw;
I've been a bit dean t' deal to-neet,
An' thowt 'at I wad caw;
What, cant'e like me, dus t'e think?
I think I wad like thee" –
"I dunnet know who't is," says I,
Says he, "It's nobbut me."

We pestit on a canny while,
I thowt his voice I kent ;
An' then I steal quite whisht away,
An' oot at t' dooer I went.
I creap, an' gat him be cwoat laps,
'Twas dark, he cuddent see;
He startit roond, an' said, "Who's that?"
Says I, "IT'S NOBBUT ME."

An' menny a time he com agean.
An' menny a time I went,
An' sed, "Who's that 'at's jiken theer?"
When gaily weel I kent:
An' mainly what t' seam answer com,
Fre back o t' laylick tree;
He sed, "I think thoo knows who't is,
Thoo knows it's nobbut me."

It's twenty year an' mair sen than,
En ups an' doons we've hed;
An' six fine barnes hev blest us beath,
Sen Jim an' me war wed.
An' menny a time I've known him steal,
When I'd yan on my knee,
Ta mak me start, an' then wad laugh –
"Ha! ha! IT'S NOBBUT ME."

# PARTY GIRL

New Year's Eve party, Bowness-on-Windermere 1960's style!

Jiving, rocking to the music
Dancers swayed and swung around
Crazed with passion for the motion
Hooked upon the beat and sound.

When all at once a striking beauty
Nubile nymph on young man's arm
Turning heads of all the dancers
Entered with magnetic charm.

Clinging shimmering silver lurex
Side-split skirt with glimpse of thigh
Overdressed but only slightly
Made poor father heave a sigh!

Skipping, jaunting, proud of sweetheart
Son smiles under father's gaze
Introduces him to girlfriend
"Pleased I'm sure," she shyly says.

Father seems somewhat uneasy
As his wife is standing by
Guests stop dancing, eyes upon him
All at once they wonder: why?

Eager son for signs of favour
Looks to one and then the other
Father dignified and stately says:
*"My girl, I knew your mother!"*

★   ★   ★

# HOW BANK VOLES DO THEIR COURTING

Dangerous when Kestrels are about!

Whilst watching Sir David Attenborough's programme on the *The Life of Birds*, I was fascinated to learn how a vole finds its way home through the long grass and how the kestrel locates its prey.

Vegetarian Bank Vole, when first leaving his hole
Does not travel by map or a compass.
There's a forest of grass through which Voley must pass
Without making a sound or a rumpus.

Voley nibbles and gnaws fresh grass in his paws
As he opens a path through the thicket
He sniffs at the air, looking here and there
For vole predators … they don't play cricket!

So he marks all his track to find his way back
By squirting his u-rine in dots
And he sets out his border of vole-law and order
Which he claims as his property lots.

The squirts which he leaves, he hopes and believes
Will find him a mate on the way
Though it means nought to me, to Miss Vole, do you see,
She sniffs of the nuptials one day!

Both smell their way back along vole-smelly track
Where they frolic in conjugal bliss!
But high up above, while they make "v-underful" love,
There's an "Awac" locked onto their piss!

Unknown to the voles, both innocent souls
Ultra-violet reflects from their u-rine
The Kestrel has ways of seeing ultra vi-o-let rays
As if they are bathed in sunshine!

So *"au moment critique"* when the Voles have gone weak
The Kestrel dives down on its prey.
That fatal food chain has claimed life again
But? There are many more voles on the way!

LH November 1998

★   ★   ★

# JOSSY EN JESSY'S COURTEN

## Finding romance at a Merry Neet

When I was a lad, farmers and their families in a community would help one another at busy times of the year e.g. at sheep shearing – clipping-time or as in this case at threshing time. The threshing process separated the corn from the sheaves to provide winter food for the family and the stock.

Prior to the invention of traction engines and tractors it was done with flails but in my youth tractors were replacing horses on the farms and they were used to power the threshing machines. Even so, there was still the need for plenty of man power to pitch sheaves from the stacks and feed the thresher, bag the corn, as well as to stack the straw for bedding and bag the chaff.

The women folk supplied the vitals and refreshments during the day and prepared taty-pot suppers for the Merry Neets which usually followed. In the evening there was live music-making dancing, singing and telling of tales. This was also an opportunity for folk to let off steam and for young folk to meet and find a mate. So it was that Jossy and Jessy got together.

Ya neet lang sen at threshen time
Efter t' thresher hed whined o day
O t' farmen folk fre roond aboot
Hed com ta help in t' ald communal way.

Efter t' wark was done – com t' merry neet ...
Thur was music, tales en sang
Us lads en lasses could find a mate
En some – didn't tak sa lang!

Thur was lots o' dancen en laiken aboot
Yam brew'd ales en strang damson gin
T' women folk thrang bringen t' taty-pot,
While we o gat sowen in.

Thur was a turble mixture o' happy folk
But oor Jossy was rayder shy
He fair wanted ta join in t' pill-dill
But felt feckless en woddn't try.

Yut oor Jossy was a fine en hansom lad
He was tow (tall) en strang en healthy
A yeoman farmer's son en heir
Yan day might be gay wealthy!

He was sweet on Jessy a sarvant lass
Wha worked on oor nebber's farm
But Jossy was slaa ut commen foret
Nut versed in romance ner charm!

When Jessy cocked her eye ut Joss
She'd felt her feelens takken  hod
But Jossy's face nobbut flushed o'er
En he could nobbut mannish a nod!

So Jessy pent up wi damson gin
Was eager ta tak her chance
Her bonny blue eyes shone breetly
As she tow'd Jossy intul t' dance.

His be-ats, like gurt post-hammers, banged aboot
Joss couldn't quite git the knack
It was back en foret en roond en roond
What! – He met hissel comen back!

But Jessy was a patient en kindly lass
She guided his beats tul t' beat
She coaxed en cuddled her man alang
Til he was starten ta enjoy his neet!

*Then Jossy started ta git a bit knack*
*O' swirlen Jess roond en leaden her back*
*He latched on tul t' rhythm en o t' fancy girations*
*Hodden Jess closer en closer, he felt new crazy sensations.*

O t' melodians en fiddles, flutes en drums
Enraptured oor merry thrang
But they paused noo en then when boss declared
That yan body wod give us a sang.

So Jossy sat doon close up tul Jessy
He'd nivver felt sae happy ner grand
As he gev her a lisle hug en smiled at her
Then gently she held his hand.

He gev it a lisle squeeze; Jess grinned at him
Her face warmed wid a gentle glow
Joss was dee-af tul t' words o' t' singer
Because Jessy was exciten him so!

Jossy plucked up his courage: Could he walk her yam?
But Jessy was coy and she looked away
Joss still hed ta larn aboot women
How they don't allus mean what they say!

Jess said she was flayt aboot boggles
En lonnin wod be dark under t' trees
But Joss said he wod hod en protect her
If happen she wus shaken at knees.

Well they walked hand in hand in t' moonleet
Aye t' shadders <u>were</u> dark under t' trees
But oor Jessy felt safe with her Jossy
So she hugged him en gev him a squeeze!

That neet fer hoors en hoors efta t' pill-dill
They walked tagither fer miles
Larnen aboot yan anudder
Happy in langings en smiles.

*On t' ald clapper brig in t' moonleet*
*Wid t' beck running clear be-laa*
*They sat theer danglen  thur legs tagither*
*Lovelorn under t' mornin' star.*

It was nobbut tethera – (three) eer efta
That Jess en Joss were wed
In them days –  courten took langer
Afoor they "took hod" en gat inta bed!

*c.* LH 10.10.2013

LH and Jean on the old clapper bridge in Bretherdale

Whilst researching my Hayton ancestors and finding out where they lived, my wife Jean and I discovered from Censuses and the Corn Rent maps that Haytons owned farms in Bretherdale in the 1700s, including Dog Lumb and Midwathstead. We found an old clapper bridge and a ford at Beckside. The clapper bridge was constructed of three long, heavy stones: two cantilevered at each side of the beck (stream) with the third stone "clapped" across the gap over the other two. I imagined Jossy and Jessy sitting there in the moonlight, having attended the threshing and the Merry Neet. That was the inspiration for the poem.

# GIRL BUNNY

This is a joke which I heard at a Merry Neet and I embellished a little and put into verse.

**Glossary:**

**A'foor** = before
**Allus** = always
**Burra** = burrow
**Doo-er** = door
**Gurt** = large
**Hard** = heard

**If you would** = if you understand
**Leeved** = lived
**Lonnin** = green lane or path
**Rayder** = rather
**Reet** = right
**Thowt** = thought

*(Part one in country bunny voice)*

I'll tell you a tale
About a girl bunny
Which I thowt when I hard it
Was rayder funny.

Girl bunny leeved
In a burra in t'wood
Beside a nice lonnin
If you would.

Noo lover boy bunny
A gurt rabbit buck
Went up t'doo-er
Ta try his luck.

He knocked on t'doo-er
She shouted "Who's there?"
"It's lover boy bunny
Wi time ta spare!"

"Come in, come in!"
She shouted with glee
For this happened quite often
Der yer see?

Well just across t'path
Sat a fine buck hare
Who watching this practice
Was driven reet spare.

He'd seen that each morning
Just aboot nine
This gurt butch bunny
Arrived allus on time.

So on t'following morning
At just a'foor nine
T'buck hare knocked on t'doo-er
En his whiskers did shine!

*(Part two in posh bunny voice)*

Girl bunny then shouted
"Who is there?"
And the usual reply
Came from the hare.

"Come in, come in!"
Girl bunny cried
It's warm and it's cosy
Here inside.

So in went the hare
And closed the door
Till along came boy bunny
Just hoping to score.

Boy bunny as usual
Thought he would knock
But on hearing the reply
He got quite a shock!

For girl bunny replied
"I've no time for you
I've got an appointment
I'm having a hare-do!!!"

*c.* LH 1980

# THE FARMER'S SON CAME RIDING
Ode to Roger and Heather Gardner on their
Silver Wedding Anniversary
(Abridged version - *Heather is my Niece*)

Ladies and Gentlemen,
Members of the Gardner and Hayton families,
Relatives, Friends and Guests

There are so many wonderful things you can say about Roger and Heather, Julia and James, John and Eva and the Gardner family.

I have been thinking about Roger's cow philosophy or his Bovine Theory of Relativity! Like Einstein, Roger does a lot of thinking – when he comes in from milking and sits on the floor by the Aga! That is Roger's place for thinking, planning and philosophising. He has a paternal ancestor, who was a very good teacher and taught my mother. So I warm to Roger's theory of relativity.

Roger tells me that there is no difference between the behaviour of cattle in a herd

Roger and Heather in playful embrace at Ullswater

and the behaviour of humans. They have natural leaders, aggressive ones, headstrong individuals, quiet ones and sexy ones! Only cattle are more honest about love-making and less complicated – Roger is quite straightforward about such things!

Now when Roger visited Kentmere over 25 years ago, I have a feeling that his theory of relativity was in its embryo stages. When he clapped eyes on Heather in her hot pants and with her long hair, he clearly saw her 'as best young heifer around!' He did not waste a lot of time.

This Silver Wedding is a milestone on what we all hope is a long journey of continued happiness for you both and for all your family and friends. We all love you – and we must tell you, Roger – your Bovine Relativity Theory works!

So now I will take you back to your courting days:

# THE FARMER'S SON CAME RIDING

The stars were bright in the firmament, as he rode the Ratherheath way
The road was a ribbon of moonlight and none would say him "Nay"!
The farmer's son came riding, riding, Honda-borne he came
And the call of the wild was beckoning that none of us can tame.

I could hear the whine of the engine as I stood in the evening cold
And the farmer's son came riding, riding, purposeful and bold
Deterred not by frost nor fingers numb but spurred by lover's zeal
His heart aflame with love's delight was all that he could feel!

He was homing to my brother's daughter under the starlit dome
Sweeping through the hills and corners like a pigeon racing home.
And the farmer's son came riding, riding, along the valley floor
Gerard's daughter cocked her ear as the sound came through the door.

There in the Brow Top kitchen doing her nightly chores
Was the girl of his dreams, listening, listening, hearing her brothers' snores
For Heather was the boys' big sister, the apple of her father's eye
Cheerful and always reliable, but her womanhood was nigh.

Above in the bedroom, now wide awake, having heard the Honda's roar
The brothers tiptoed, tiptoed, and closed the bedroom door:
Edwin, George and Jonathon like young throstles in a nest
Leaned out of Brow Top window clad only in their vests.

For the farmer's son was Roger – and "Rodge" was coming now
And Dad he was a-milking, milking, milking every cow.
"Roger is coming to see Heather! Here he comes now!
And Dad he's still a-milking, milking every cow!"

And the farmer's son came riding, riding, up to the farmhouse door
And Heather, shy like Granny, excited, was washing the kitchen floor
Restraining her longing by doing things, but lost to the thrill in her breast
The farmer's son came knocking, knocking; and all of us know the rest!

The Toast is for Good Health and for Long and
Happy Lives Together!

TO ROGER AND HEATHER

LH  12.02.1997

# ODE TO JOY, A REAL WOMAN
## My tribute to my late wife Joy on her 60th birthday

Woman to a man is a puzzlement
Not capable of definition
Yet Man begotten, beguiled and bemused
Is sculpted, fashioned, moulded and used

An innocent pawn; devoid of suspicion.

Woman is not a female man
A different species altogether
As brave as a lioness protecting her pride
And proud as a peacock with a man by her side

But as changeable as the weather!

Woman to man is a puzzlement
She has dominion over him
A femme fragile as porcelain; a damsel delicate as a petal
Can inspire him to greatness or fire up his fettle

Simply by exposing a limb!

Woman is not a female man
She is far and away more clever
Proud Man the hunter, Man the leader
She makes Man her lover and Man her feeder

Then with love and care rewards his endeavour.

★     ★     ★

These things I have learned in the last twelve years
Since our mid-life crises I've recovered my spurs
Joy, you love the evenings while I love the morn
You get up at six, but I wake at dawn.

So I rise as the birds sing at a quarter past five
When all systems are go and I feel most alive
But I've learned at my peril, I must not wake you
So I work on my computer or read in the loo!

You've taught me to be tidy and take off each shoe
Lest the leaves or the muck are carted all through
I hang up my clothes now, which you iron with zeal
Of the benefits and burdens I'm getting the feel.

I'm a qualified shopper, I've got the highest award
As you sample each garment, I've learned not to be bored
I comment on style, on colour and tone
To avoid "I shouldn't have bought it" the usual moan!

Now I'm so accomplished in feminine fashion and style
If you buy when I'm absent, I have only to smile
My frown now a saving, you rarely buy without me
My only budget sanction's a frown, do you see?

But my Lioness you're loving and caring as well
Any threat to my wellbeing you would banish to hell
"Have you had your tablets? Have you got your spray?"
Is your primary concern at both ends of the day.

What matters the price of a hairdo or perm
When my Jollity is with me to extend my life's term?
You are young, you are fit, you are fun, you are free
Your love is sincere for both our families and me.

You're a tease and a tomboy, a devil may care
Concerned for appearance and styling your hair
But practical, sensible: Yes, you've got it all
Beside you with pride "your little fat Man" walks tall!

★   ★   ★

But still Joy to me: you're a puzzlement
You show no signs of wear
Your sixty years don't show at all
You are still so young and fair.

I am sure you're not a female man
Of that I am most certain
But that evidence is my evidence
Which remains behind the curtain!

I give you the toast: my Wife, my Joy
The centre of life to "Our Boy"
Good health, long life and happiness too
Together in love we'll see it through.

Happy Birthday to my lovely "Joy, Jollity or Joyous"

LH 17.1.2003

# *NOSTALGIA AND MY OLD MG

Those times in youth we treasure still
When on a sunlit day
With oil up to the elbows
Beneath some sump we lay.

Perhaps we bought our pride and joy
From Andy Murphy's yard
Scrap cars were limousines to us
We'd labour on them hard.

At first no thought of women
Obscured our concentration
Every minute then was spent
To improve the acceleration!

We did overtime with constant zeal
To pay for our jalopy
Mention then of courting
Was thought a little soppy!

But from time to time some girl would come
Perhaps to help in cleaning
Maybe we noticed now and then
When she was closely leaning –

That she had curves and headlamps too
Perhaps acceleration
Then our feelings for the car
Were tinged with a new sensation –

As in those lowly parts of man
Where passion ebbs and flows
And love, confused with nature
Overcomes the doubts and no's.

So then: how to impress her?
Let's find a red MG
To speed through blossomed lanes in spring
Just my lovely girl and me.

Do you remember those happy times of youth?
Yes, the images are clear and strong
Nights of stars and moonlight
As enraptured we bowled along.

She was a car and she was a girl
We were out in our old TD
Yes me with my arm round her shoulder
And she with her hand on my knee.

Now you with your cars historic
Which you cherish as I would too
Give some thought to this conundrum:
Was it the car, or was it the girl,
Or the memory of the two?

* Lake District Historic Car Club. LH 24.01.1983

My Girl Jean and the MG with tin cans – courtesy of our guests – which jangled all the way home after our wedding

# THE MAGIC OF THE INTERNET

After losing Joy in 2007 all my friends encouraged me to be positive. *Dum vivimus viviamus et gaudeamus:* while we live, let us live and be joyful. So in March 2010 I took a deep breath and decided to try the internet. I joined the *Guardian Soulmates* website.

After entering my profile and a description of the person I was looking for, I pressed the key for the best matches. Jean's profile came to the top with a 91 per cent match – and she was living only 18 miles away! Eventually we met for our first date ... and the rest, as they say, is history.

# A WHIRLWIND ROMANCE WITH MY JEANIE

I saw your smile on "Soulmates"
And I hoped it wasn't too late
Over 90% compatible,
Your credentials were impeccable
… And so we arranged a date.

Wow! Since then the world has altered
My will has never faltered
You occupy the centre of my world
You warm me to my toes like sunshine upon a rose
Stirs its petals to be so gloriously unfurled.

Words cannot en-capture the ecstasy or rapture
We shared together through those lovely sunlit days
Your sweetness and your gentleness
The quiet application of your loveliness
Expressed beautifully in so many ways!

Then on the pillion of my Moto Guzzi
Not weak-willed, lily-livered or fuzzy
You're a natural cuddly biker kind of Gal!
With your gentle arms around me
In our "Seventh Heaven" you have found me
You're my Angel, you're my Baby, you're my Pal!

LH 6.40 a.m. 22nd March 2010

# SPARKLE RHYTHM

## My Internet Girl

Jean's chosen internet name was "Sparkle Rhythm". The title caught my eye and I liked the sound of "Sparkle Rhythm". I was not to be disappointed when we met!

We became engaged a fortnight after our first meeting and were married four months later. This poem was written for Jean a few days after we got engaged.

Somewhere up there, above the Cosmos
Somewhere there is a guiding hand
But when cancer took my Jollity from me
I was sorely tried to understand.

Yet through all the pain and grief
Throughout the loneliness and sorrow
My Family, my Friends and Jesus
Brought me hope of a new tomorrow.

Now that new tomorrow is here today
My Jean has consented to be my Wife
Loving, caring, selfless and sincere
Jean brings her special sparkle to my life.

LH 2010

It quickly became clear to me that my fiancée was held in high esteem by those who knew her, and that her work as a specialist nurse in South Lakeland was very highly regarded. Before becoming a nurse, Jean was a teacher for ten years.

Jean has had great experience of learning, reading and the enjoyment of the English language and our culture. Her steady hand and dogged perseverance in the editing and indexing of our first book *The Collected Tales of a Lakeland Lad* was fundamental to its completion. We gathered together the jottings and verses I had done over the years. I have never worked with anyone with such determination. She inspires me. I could not have achieved this without her.

# A "GORGEOUS" SPRING 2010

In the spring and early summer of 2010 Jean and I were invited to meet her friends and mine. It was lovely to know that they all cared. Our match was celebrated and we were made welcome wherever we went.

This was a period of getting to know each other and doing things together. Jean embraced my interests and I hers. I found I could take her anywhere. Her kindness and caring nature shone refreshingly like the morning sun wherever we went.  At Easter I wrote this ode to Jean.

# TO MY JEAN – AN EASTER ODE

Wherever I take you
Wherever I go
Your smiles are infectious
My friends they all know
That my heart is inspired
And my face is aglow.

Aglow with the love light
You spark in my eyes
Aglow with the knowledge
That you're gentle and wise
Yet teenage excitement
Thrills us all through
With wild wonderful thrills
In the things that we do.

Your kisses are gentle
Your kisses are divine
Like swift shafts of lightning
They thrill through my spine
You are young and so vibrant
My years melt away
As I awake in your arms
At the dawn of the day.

Selfless care you have given throughout your life
Selfless caring precluded your being a wife
Yet now in our autumn you come to me
A creature so perfect, yet you don't seem to see

How lovely you are
How attractive your ways
That I just want to love and protect you
For the rest of my days.

Jean you are special
Jean you are great
We must not waste a moment
Our love it won't wait
It is twenty one days since we first met
And each new day is better yet!

LH  Easter Day 2010

★    ★    ★

During the period from Easter until our wedding on July 23rd 2010, we attended a variety of meetings in which I am involved, including the Lakeland Dialect Society. Jean was a member of Cartmel Choral Society and we enjoyed their concert in Cartmel Priory, as well as the International Music Festival concerts in Ulverston, directed by the renowned pianist, Anthony Hewitt.

I introduced Jean to motor cycling. She had reservations at first because of her experience of nursing young men on the orthopaedic ward after their motorbike accidents and fracturing their femurs. I found that she rode pillion on my Moto Guzzi as a natural. The sense of freedom and the sensation of the open air seemed to thrill her and she glowed with the new experience.

Jean after her first ride on the Moto Guzzi

We visited the VMCC Motor Cycle Show in Stafford where my friend Bill Bewley won "Best in Show" with his Vincent Black Shadow. When I rang the next day to congratulate Bill on his achievement, I said that Jean and I thought we must have brought him good luck, because I had introduced Jean to Bill and his wife Jenny at their home on our second date and we had our first kiss beside his highly polished motorbike in the garage. Bill asked me if we had noticed the bike's registration number: LOV 579. Quick as lightning Jean responded by adding the 5, 7 and 9 together to make 21, which two numerals added together make 3. She laughed as she pointed out that 3 is a backwards E, thus making the LOV into LOVE! That really was fun with numbers!

In May 2010 we helped together on the gates of the showground at the Westmorland County Agricultural Society's "Country Fest" – a lovely day. We attended other agricultural events, farm meetings and the Geldard's Barbecue at Low Foulshaw Farm - all of which Jean took in her stride. We also had an enjoyable day at Chester Races with Reg Gifford.

In June 2010 our friends Jenny Bewley and Jen Sansom held a joint birthday cruise on Windermere. The evening was warm with just a light rain and the lake was calm. The guests had a wonderful time with an excellent buffet on board. There was a jazz band playing, so Jean and I did a "Kentmere Reel"! It was lovely for me to introduce her to so many friends but hard for Jean to remember everyone's names.

We attended Levens Church where Jean was made very welcome and we joined other church members at a service in Carlisle Cathedral. Jean accompanied me and helped with my talks at various celebration events. She was supportive, not only on happy occasions, but sad ones too. When my old friend Ernest Shepherd died, Wendy his widow asked me to do the eulogy at his funeral. We visited Wendy on the day he died and Jean was a real comfort and help to both of us.

In June 2010 Jean and I wrote and performed together "A Prayer for Today" for the Lakeland Dialect Service in Levens Church. The Lakeland Dialect Society holds a service every two years in a different church in Cumbria each time. The whole service is in Lakeland dialect including the hymns and the sermon. Everyone interested is welcome to attend. Later that month we helped with the Levens Open Gardens Day.

Although I enjoy much of the same music as Jean, I discovered that she has a wider knowledge and appreciation than my own and she has delighted in introducing me to music that is new to me. As well as her involvement with choral music, she has a special love of Beethoven and Chopin, as I do too.

Between organising our wedding and attending many social events, we had an enormously happy and busy time. I remain totally amazed that my fiancée took up the mantle so completely and enriched both our lives with quiet accomplishment in such a short period of time. It seemed magic and still does.

Jean arriving for our wedding at Levens Church with Jan Tomson, matron of honour, and her cousin Derek Steel, who gave her away

# A VALENTINE

Oh woe is me and lack-a-day
I languish in guilt as W.S Gilbert might say
For on the fourteenth of Feb most ladies swoon
And expect pink cards delivered before high noon!

Research indicates this old custom began
On the festival of Valentine – a saintly Italian man
In 1450 they drew their lovers by lots
And one hundred years later they printed love knots.

This shy country lad as I've always been
Finds it hard to select a card fit for his Queen!
For my lady fair of countenance high
Has no equal now nor in days gone by!

I alone have the measure of my perfect girl
You shiver my timbers and put my head in a whirl
Yet this I can't find on any Valentine creation
There is nothing to grace you: I've searched the nation.

So please accept this folded page
'Twas a Valentine practice from age to age
Your name appears inscribed by me
As was the custom in fifteen fifty three.

★   ★   ★

For love is eternal, love is divine
No professor of philosophy can its nature define
Yet you and I only our special love can know
For all lovely couples have their own unique "glow".

*YOUR VALENTINE*

LH  14.2.2012

# 3

# A COUNTRY LAWYER'S TALES

My legal career in Lakeland and afar spans the period from October 1957 to October 2008 which commenced with 5 years' Articles of Apprenticeship. Initially I had the guiding influence of my late brother Jack, who died in 1967, and my Principal, Kenneth Jackson. At Blackpool College of Law where I studied for my intermediate law exams I met my lifelong friends, Reg Ashworth and Michael Winkley. My friendship and legal partnership with Michael Winkley, which lasted 35 years, was the basis from which the practice expanded, taking in Tony James and Malcolm Whiteside followed by Peter Briggs, Andrew Bromley, Keith Wood, John Oldroyd, Naomi Fell and Patricia Sanderson. We employed some very talented assistant solicitors and we also trained articled clerks.

As the practice expanded, so did our wonderful team of support staff at each office. Having started as an office boy myself at the beginning of my articles I had some idea how they felt when later the pressure was on and my priorities changed during the day. I could also be tiresome, as Jean Cowling so colourfully portrays in her verse to me on my 60th birthday!

I was a general practitioner and dealt with a wide variety of human problems and aspirations. Conveyancing was the bread and butter of the practice then but I acted for an increasing number of hoteliers and tourist businesses as the practice grew in Windermere. This involved work connected with the re-development in the 1970s of

LH working on a case at home.

Bowness Bay, and legal work for businesses based on Lake Windermere and in the southern lakes. This work continued and expanded throughout my career and brought me in contact with a variety of entrepreneurial clients. These are the people who create work and employment for others, seeing and taking opportunities. I enjoyed being an adviser to them but I always remained independent.

Until Tony James took over most of the Magistrates' Court work to allow me to do more commercial work, I dealt with the court work. I appeared in Windermere, Kendal, Shap, Hawkshead and Ambleside Magistrates' Courts. Yes, there were Courts in all those places and the Magistrates served their communities well because they had local knowledge. They looked for ways to help offenders to solve their problems rather than send them to prison, which often proves to be a college for further crime. However, they could also be tough. The Magistrates' Clerks were sticklers for ensuring any solicitor appearing in their courts had done their homework and prepared the cases properly. Some of my stories come from that period.

I was always quite shy as a young man and so I decided to do a series of advocacy training courses to equip me to appear on behalf of clients in our Magistrates' Courts. For about 7 years I did most of the appearances for our firm, Hayton Winkley, in court on behalf of defendants.

Work in the Magistrates' Courts also involved road traffic accidents, alcohol licensing for local hotels, pubs and restaurants, as well as family disputes and claims for maintenance, usually held in afternoon Courts. I developed a reputation for the thorough examination of the facts in each case. Later I occasionally acted for the Police in prosecuting some of their cases before the Crown Prosecution Service was formed.

# THE BURGLAR

## and

## Courage in the Moonlight!

My first case prosecuting for the Police – long before the CPS (Crown Prosecution Service) was formed – concerned a burglary at a house just out of Windermere on the Crook road.

Two elderly spinsters lived alone on a smallholding out of town. One bred pedigree goats – she had a large Billy goat on stud to which we later took our goats. The other sister bred fell ponies. Both of them were self-reliant and courageous ladies with the strong spirit of country folk, as I will relate.

★　★　★

The moon shone bright through the window<br>
The house was cold and still<br>
As the silhouette of the Burglar<br>
Slid over the window sill.

His car was parked on the country road
As the Police patrol went by
So our constable noted the number
It was good policing – that's why.

The fibres from his coat on the drain pipe
Were found the very next day
But there he was now in the bedroom
Where the sleeping old lady lay.

She rose from her bed as a warrior
Would rise on a night attack
But her armour was only her nightwear
With nothing to shield her back.

The sheets of the bed in the moonlight
Exploded before his eyes
As her courage and dauntless spirit
Took the Burglar by surprise.

He leapt over the bed and took to his heels
With the old lady in hot pursuit
And such was his haste he dropped the lot
And escaped without his loot.

Her sister was also awakened
And she joined in the hue and cry
She launched herself at the Burglar
As the dark-clad thief sped by.

But he escaped into dark shadows
Cast over the country lane
A car engine roared in the distance
The Burglar was free again.

When at half past two in the morning
The Police knocked upon his door
"He's been in bed with me all night"
Said his wife of common law.

"So who's been out in the car then?
For the engine still is hot
And I've the number on my clip board list
So you're talking Tommy Rot!"

In the end at the old Quarter Sessions
He pleaded guilty to his crime
Justice was done, no violence
But he had to serve his time.

The ladies lived on with their animals
But their windows and doors were barred
For crime is a cancer of freedom
Which leaves all humanity scarred.

# THE LAKELAND CLEARANCES

When I opened the Windermere office of Hayton Winkley in 1964, I received instructions from many of my school friends at Windermere Grammar School who were brought up in Windermere, Ambleside and the villages and hamlets in the valleys of Lakeland. They were having to move out of their native areas to the town of Kendal. Housing development was mainly around Kendal and even further afield and workshops were mainly on the industrial estates and not in their local communities. I would call this time "the Lakeland clearances". A lot of my work was in trying to get planning consent for workshops and homes in Lakeland, but the rigidity of the planning policies precluded any real success.

The planning legislation of 1947, while desirable to protect visual amenity, had an effect partly similar to the Scottish clearances. Though very necessary to protect the visual amenity of Lakeland, it created a frustrating and unbalanced system. This brought me into contention, on behalf of clients, with the Planning Board. There was no "Use Class" for holiday homes. House prices rocketed when outside buyers of holiday homes outbid the locals.

If it had been necessary under a special 'Use Class' to apply for planning consent for holiday use, the Board could have looked at each community and kept a balance.

We welcomed new people coming into the communities because they often brought energy and new ideas. They also brought capital and created work, which was good for Lakeland, but there was no mechanism to keep a balance in each area or to consider the needs of the local economy in the planning process. It was the lack of balance and blinkered thinking which created the more recent "Homes for Locals" campaigns, none of which have really remedied the problem.

During the crucial early years when young families were moving out of the villages and could not afford homes there, planning consents for small workshops were also very difficult indeed to obtain. All this made work for me but the policies caused me heartache when I saw local people having to buy houses in Kendal only to travel back to work in the Lake District villages. Short-term and short-sighted policies have done nothing for "Global Warming" or the preservation of fossil fuel!

As a local businessman I was asked to address *The Future of Rural Cumbria Conference* in November 1989. In part my paper was a lament for the loss of our customs and usages and the lack of opportunity for young artisans to have small workshops and likewise their homes within their local community. This meant that consequently school numbers declined and many village schools closed, which all had a lasting effect on the character of the countryside. There was much talk about the socio-economic aspects but little was done.

# ADOPT, ADAPT, IMPROVE

In 1964 I also joined Windermere, Ambleside and District Round Table and got involved on the steering and fundraising committee, when we decided on the ambitious project of building the Marchesi Centre. This gave me my first involvement with charity law in drafting the constitution and dealing with the connected legal issues. I learned much from my days in Round Table, working with an excellent group of capable and enthusiastic young business and professional men, who wanted to give something more to their community. I have always admired the aims and objectives of the Round Table movement which are as follows:

1. To develop the acquaintance of young men through the medium of their various occupations.
2. To emphasise the fact that one's calling offers an excellent medium of service to the community.
3. To cultivate the highest ideals in business, professional and civic traditions.
4. To recognise the worthiness of all legitimate occupations and to dignify, each his own, by precept and example.
5. To further the establishment of peace and goodwill in international relationships.
6. To further these objects by meetings, lectures, discussions and other activities.

I also found the Round Table Grace inspiring as it expresses succinctly the ideals which one tries to live up to.

### THE ROUND TABLE GRACE

May we O Lord adopt thy creed,

Adapt our ways to serve thy need,

And we who on thy bounty feed,

Improve in thought and word and deed.

The life of a country lawyer is never dull, neither is it always easy. All sorts of conflicts of interest can arise between clients and friends. My genial boss, Kenneth Jackson, used to say: "You have to have a hide like a rhinoceros and the wisdom of Solomon to be a solicitor!"  I am not sure I achieved either but I know what he meant.

Being a farmer's son and enjoying some hobby farming with my first wife, Sandra, I developed a degree of specialism in agricultural law. This widened my experience, took me abroad and later involved me in the work of the Westmorland County Agricultural Society.

In later years I dealt with inheritance and estate planning, capital taxation, probate and administration of wills – many of which I had drafted for clients years before.

I have been blessed with partners and colleagues who have been a pleasure to work with. I have had many interesting and loyal clients who became good friends. You all know who you are. This book cannot include or do justice to all of you but it is a celebration of the happy times we have had in work and play together. Thank you.

After the poem *What Does a Lawyer Do?* there follow some of my experiences along the way. I have deliberately changed the names of the people and places involved, where necessary, to maintain confidentiality. Client privilege and confidentiality rules prevent me from disclosing many of the fascinating and amusing cases with which I have dealt. Some cases have been in the public domain and in others consent has been given by the client.

★   ★   ★

# WHAT DOES A LAWYER DO?
## Justice or hearsay?

All professions are criticised at one time or another but lawyers are often blamed for the ills of the world; yet the same folk will tell you: *"My lawyer is a grand chap"*. To have a friend who is a lawyer can be a benefit in life.

One question which often comes up is: *"How can you defend in Court someone whom you know is guilty?"*

In answer to this I usually ask the questioner to imagine him or herself accused, arrested and placed in custody for a crime of which he or she has no knowledge and is innocent. You will need help from a trained lawyer whom you can trust.

Everyone under English law is presumed innocent unless and until proved guilty. Trial by the media is not just; neither is trial by a mob.

My job as a lawyer is not to be the judge and jury but to ascertain the facts from the accused, check the evidence against the accused and make necessary enquiries as to the facts surrounding the case. My duty is to place those facts truthfully before the Court. I must not mislead the Court.

If in the investigation the accused admits his guilt, then I would advise the accused to plead guilty and put all mitigation available before the Court. However, there are all manner of difficult cases where an innocent person admits to a crime, believing it is simpler to do so or because he/she thinks no one will believe him or her. There may also be outside influences and fear of reprisals. That is why under a fair system of justice we all have a part to play in the process.

The poem *What Does a Lawyer Do?* touches on the role of lawyers in society. Sadly, in today's world with the advent of monetarism, legal aid has been cut by successive governments, which limits the time for thorough investigation and proper representation. Many Magistrates' Courts have been closed, so decisions are taken out of the community, creating travel problems and difficulties in communication with the accused. The professional duty is to put the clients' interests first but centralisation and specialisation in larger, distant towns and cities are depriving our communities of local expertise.

★ ★ ★

# WHAT DOES A LAWYER DO?

You ask me what does a lawyer do?
I sigh: where to begin?
Law libraries are full of legal tomes
That encompass human sin.

Where two or more folk come together
Some rule they will devise
While one means this, another that
Disputes will soon arise.

The law of the wild and nature's law
Have endured since time began
While we attempt to civilise
In the written words of man.

Such words may be enacted
Authorised by Royal nod
To some such acts are sacrosanct
As if the words of God.

While others heed them not at all
Transgress the common law
As greed, aggression, sex and hate
Are pursued by tooth and claw.

All shades of such behaviour
Appear in the book of life
From the worthless pursuit of materialism
To the marriage with a wife.

Well someone drafts the rules we need
Someone must say what they mean
For a mob will condemn on the words of another
Who says what a third has seen.

Someone must care for freedom
See fairness and justice done
Let fair play shine in the affairs of man
Like the warming rays of the sun.

Someone must hear the prisoner's tale
Someone must put his case
Even if he is guilty
The judge must see his face.

Someone must know what his rights are
Those rights we all assume
The justice our forefathers fought for
The equality we all presume!

That someone may be your lawyer
That someone may be you
Sitting as one of the noble twelve
Jurors good and true.

Solicitor, Barrister, Judge and Clerk
Magistrate and Jury-man
All of these folk are just folk like you
Balancing JUSTICE the best they can.

© LH 1982

# SHEEP TRESPASS OR WAS IT?
## Look for the evidence before it goes cold

**Glossary**

**T'Bobby** = Policeman
**Cam stanes** = wall topping stones
**Caps langcrown** = is beyond belief or very puzzling
**Crack or good crack** = a chat or good conversation
**Hubbyshoo** = trouble or controversy, a commotion or noisy gathering
**Laiken** = playing

**Lile lasses** = little girls
**Lowp** = jump
**Maaen guss** = mowing grass.
**Meedas** = meadows
**Proven** or **proggin** = animal food
**Stown** = stolen
**Swardles** = Swaledale sheep
**Woes** = walls
**Yows** = ewes

"Fotty five of mi best swardles hev bin hijacked," said Willie. "What mun we dew aboot it? T'Bobby rang me first thing this mornin ta tell me that them new folk at caravan site hed gitten mi yows. I exed him, 'What dust ta mean? Hev they stown them or what?'

"Well t'Bobby tells me they've ivvery reet, under some damned Animals Act that oor daft Parliament hes passed, ta tak em and hod em up, provided they give em proven and watter. Is that reet?" asked Willie.

"Yes, the Animal Act has introduced a new remedy for animal trespass," I told him. "They can take them away and hold them until you pay the cost of any damage caused, provided they notify the police and give them food and water.

"Worse than that, they can claim damages and there is no straight forward way under the Act to defend their action. Challenging the amount of the claim is also difficult. We can start an action to recover goods but it will take too long. They can charge you the cost of the damage to their trees and the cost of keeping the sheep. It is a very effective remedy for sheep trespass if it is genuine. You are in a weak position. How did the sheep get into the site?" I asked. "What are they claiming? What happened?"

"Well," said Willie. "They tell me that mi sheep hev itten a turble deal o' young trees which they'd hed ta plant as a screen fer o thur damned caravans en sick-like. They've telt ma that t'claim will be aboot a thoosand pund. Well thoo knaas, it's a gay cheek. I've nivver bin against folk comen inta t'country ta relax, but there's nay give en tak wi these folk.

"Yer knaa t'visitors lowp o'er mi woes. They knock cams inta mi maaen-guss and trample o o'er meedas and nut by mi leave. They chuck beer tins en bottles aboot en kids laik in t'pastures. Well I put up wi that en o sick-like. Noo I don't mind t'lile lads en lasses enjoyen thursels en laiken aboot in oor fields but this cap's langcrown!

"Many a time I've stopped en hed a crack wid em. Aye, en I've laiked a bit o' football, kicken t'bo aboot wid em, just ta mek em welcome. En this is t'thanks I git. Well noo Leonard, thoo mun dew summat aboot it. I want mi ald yows back!

"I can't think where t'yows have gitten oot," said Willie. "Mi woes en fences er o in good order. I've always believed in fencen weel against mi nebbers. It maks fer good nebbers. O t'cam stanes er on t'wall tops. I can't think hoo this hes happened. It's a mystery ta me.

"I've allus minded mi arn business en I've nivver hed a hubbyshoo like this afoor."

It turned out that the land next to the caravan site was some distance from Willie's house and Willie had been away a few days at the time. I suggested that we arranged to meet on site at once and check the walls and fences with the Claimant. I invited the Claimant's solicitor and his Client to join us in the field from which the sheep had escaped.

Willie was right. There was no sign of walls down or poor fences. There was no place for the sheep to have escaped. We walked the boundary wall towards the far end, over a knoll and on towards a copse.

I had been looking for sheep trods in the grass and as we rounded a bend in the wall there was a concentration of feet marks behind the wall which led on round the corner. Some yards further on, out of sight to the normal view of the field, was an old gateway. This had connected the fields before the caravan site was developed. The gateway was blocked by a fairly new hurdle-type gate which was chained and padlocked.

It was then I noticed that the sheep trods converged and ran under the gate. There was a concentration of sheep foot marks showing clearly the path taken by the sheep into the caravan site. I said nothing. I had walked ahead of the rest. They were arguing with Willie about the extent of the tree damage as they followed me.

I climbed over the gate and immediately saw a long mark in the grass behind the wall. It was a yellow mark. I measured its length with my feet. I looked up as the opposition looked over the gate, their faces full of confidence.

Then I pointed to the yellow mark in the grass. The colour in their faces drained away and faded to a pale ashen hue. The yellow mark was the length of the bottom rail of the gate where the gate had been leaned against the wall! It was obvious that the gateway had been open and the gate propped against the wall while Willie was away. It appeared to have been done to allow the caravan site visitors to gain easy access to the fell as a short cut across Willie's land. The colour of the mark in the grass indicated the gate had rested there for a few days. The caravan site owner or his employees had forgotten to put the gate back and the sheep had got in as a result! The truth was written fair on the Claimant's face. It was a try-on.

I addressed the Claimant's solicitor: "You can return our sheep now please at no cost to Willie. I will send you a bill for my fee.

"I suggest Willie, if you want to let them use this gate for access to the fell, that you have me draw up a licence agreement and that they pay an annual licence fee. Furthermore they must accept responsibility for keeping the gate shut and the sheep out." The tables were turned.

Willie, a happy and satisfied client

# THE ALCOHOLIC

Through the door came an elegant lady
Refined, clearly well brought up
When I offered her tea to calm her nerves
She looked chic as she held her cup.

"My dear Mr Hayton I'm dreadfully worried,"
She uttered as she started to cry
When she passed me the charge sheet
I got my first whiff
So that was the reason why!

The breathalyser had not been invented
The charge sheet alleged: driving in drink
"But oh Mr Hayton I've given it up
Will they withdraw do you think?"

The facts when I checked them could not be denied
But she insisted she'd given up drink
"My reformed situation; please plead mitigation
Will I lose my licence do you think?"

She was a widow who grieved for her man
She drank to soothe her pain
Medical help I arranged for her
Lest she did it all over again.

In the Court she looked so elegant
She faced the charge with style
As she walked into the witness box
She wore a charming smile.

She took the oath with dignity
She could have been a Queen
Looked straight in the eye of the Magistrate
The most convincing I had seen.

Her sadness in bereavement
Alcohol became her prop
Now medical help had taught her
Not to touch another drop.

I cannot remember her punishment
But still clearly I recall
How outside the Court just afterwards
As she stood there proud and tall

She fumbled in her handbag
Then looking sheepish in her sin
She produced and drank from a bottle
Long slugs of London Gin!

★   ★   ★

© LH *c.*1970

# "CONTRACT RACE!
# WHAT IS A CONTRACT RACE?"

A charming couple, near retiring age, approached my desk and I greeted the new clients with courtesy and anticipation. Both were smiling from ear to ear: the kind of smile which thinly overlays a desire to jump for joy and pour out a pent-up enthusiasm. They restrained themselves long enough to identify themselves and go through the preliminaries. Then it all came out.

He was a civil engineer and his wife a linguist. They had never really managed to settle anywhere as the job of building roads, bridges and large civil engineering works around the world, had taken them to a variety of countries. "But now we are going to settle in the Lake District. We were both born in Westmorland and we are coming home. We have just agreed to purchase this."

He dropped a glossy estate agent's brochure on my desk. It described a large 'gentleman's house' in fifteen acres of gardens, woodland, out-buildings and all the facilities we lesser mortals might dream of owning. It was a gem. They were justifiably delighted. They were both keen gardeners, ornithologists and lovers of wildlife in our area.

As with all property transactions, big or small, the lawyer needs to take basic steps to protect the clients' interest. So began the questions. There was no house to sell but how was the purchase to be financed? That was easily dealt with. Was it to be bought in joint names and how, as between them, was it to be held? We discussed the description, boundaries, services, access and all the usual matters which have to be checked. We agreed to meet on site when the draft contract was received. Normally it might be expected in about a week from the initial negotiation.

They were not in a hurry to move in. It seemed at that point a straight forward 'run of the mill' job. All appeared normal and we could make progress in a sensible and orderly way. But just as the clients stood up to go, the question came!

"WHAT IS A CONTRACT RACE?" It hit me like a brick in the face. "Why do you ask?" I replied rather abruptly. "Well," spluttered the client, "Is it important?" "Why do you ask?" I repeated.

"Well, it was just the agent said there was a contract race and I wondered what he meant."

I said, "Why didn't you tell me that first?" I suggested that they sit down again. I quickly picked up the phone and spoke to the agent.

"Yes, there is another offer for this property. The seller has been mucked about by a previous prospective buyer. Now there are two more prospective buyers who want it and your client is one. He's not going to choose the wrong one this time. The seller has decided to issue two contracts, one to each prospective buyer. The first person to exchange contracts and pay the 10% deposit will get it." So now I knew the seriousness of our position.

We had no contract in hand to sign. This was an unregistered title and searches needed to be done in the Local Authority Charges register and in the Land Charges registers. This process would normally take about two weeks. The property needed to be surveyed. The title or ownership had to be verified.

Fortunately my clients had the money available to buy the property. I did not need to worry about that as I would in some cases. I needed to check the boundaries and services against the plan and the deeds. I needed to check the title and make sure we would be paying the purchase price to the true owner and that we were not buying subject to a mortgage or a prior overriding interest. Being an unregistered title, the deeds would need to be examined and checked carefully. Normally such investigation would take between ten days and a month, depending on whether information is available and on the local authority's response time.

"Who is the seller's solicitor?" I asked. The agent gave me the name of a firm in Cardiff, South Wales! "That's a hell of a way," I thought, but said nothing. My brain was already working on a strategy for the race which was to come. How does the seller's solicitor intend to be fair to both parties? Has he already issued the other contract? Is the contract ready? When will the seller complete? Where is the other party's solicitor?" I shot these questions at the agent over the phone in staccato.

"Well," said the agent, "I believe the solicitor is preparing a contract as we speak and is going to post two copies to each of the two prospective purchasers' solicitors tonight. They will be issued at the same time in the post and the first contract to be signed on the seller's solicitor's desk will get the property. I believe the other solicitor is in Manchester. It's a big firm."

Then the agent started to pull my leg. "You haven't a hope, Len. He got started two days ago on the preliminaries and he's got a head start. They are a big firm. A lile country lad like thee? No chance!"

The agent was well known to me and was enjoying himself. I had often acted the slow country lad approach to my advantage in the past but here he was putting me on my mettle. There was a good commission in it for him and he wanted to see the contract signed. It was a seller's market, but the seller had been put to a lot of trouble by a previous would-be buyer who had said he was a cash buyer – when it was not so.

The clients had listened to this exchange with puzzlement and rising alarm. I put the phone down and appraised them of their position. I rang the firm in Cardiff. It was 10.30 a.m. Yes the contract was being typed. It would be in tonight's post. I asked if he was keeping a copy to make sure he would have one to sign. "Of course," he replied, rather haughtily.

The contract could not be faxed because fax machines had not been invented then. So how was I to do all my searches and get the signed contract on to his desk ahead of our rivals?

While my clients looked on bewildered, I gave instructions to my secretary to prepare the search forms for Keith Wood (my very able articled clerk and trainee solicitor) to attend and make a personal search of the registers at the council office in Kendal. I made the necessary arrangements with the registries to expedite the search. I despatched Keith with instructions to report to me by phone that afternoon.

I gathered the necessary forms of enquiry into my brief case. The clients were warming to the competition and were highly motivated. The property was empty, the previous owner having died. We left the office, attended on site with the sale particulars and plan. We inspected the boundaries, services and appearance of the property. I then despatched an efficient surveyor with instructions to inspect at once and to report on the condition of the house and outside buildings later that day.

I arranged with the seller's solicitor to have a copy of the contract and title available at his office in Cardiff and indicated that my clients would pick it up later in the day, in case the posted copy went astray or did not arrive in time. I did not at that stage say I was accompanying the clients. The solicitor had not heard from our rival. I asked him if he felt obliged to inform our rival's solicitor of my request. He said that all they had undertaken was to issue two contracts in the post at the same time, and whoever signed and exchanged a contract first would be the buyer. It was up to each party how they undertook the race. That seemed fair to me.

I explained my plan to my anxious clients and they readily concurred. We resolved to drive to Cardiff at once.

I shall always remember that drive. I am a bad passenger but the husband drove like a man inspired to win the Formula One world championship! A quiet, competent but determined driver, he had the bit between his teeth. He clearly intended to win that race. For my part I always assume my rival is ahead and the driver had the same thing in mind. If our opposition had the same idea then we knew they had a head start. They would be starting from Manchester while we had started from Windermere.

The clients' car was a large Ford Granada estate and I fancy we were flying most of the way. Certainly we were in Cardiff long before the office closing time with no stops.

We were ushered into the senior partner's empty room, which was the only room available for our use. The senior partner was, we were told, "in the House". He was a Welsh M.P., rather famous for his oratory and colourful clothing.

I sat judge-like in his sumptuous leather chair while my clients and I perused the title deeds. We checked the plan against the deeds, followed the devolution of ownership through the title documents down to the seller and checked that he had a good right to sell. We checked the enforceability of covenants, rights and easements.

We then checked through the contract and its terms, all of which were acceptable. We could not alter any basic terms because that would have been unfair to the other prospective buyer and it would have obliged the seller's solicitor to inform him of the change. That would have given him notice that we were ahead.

I telephoned the surveyor who provided a useful and satisfactory report. Keith telephoned and reported positively on his search enquiries. Only a control of advertisements order (common to most of the Lake District National Park) was revealed by the search. There were no charges in the register. There was nothing risky about the property.

We had been through all the pre-contract enquiries and my clients were eager to get signed up. They signed and we exchanged contracts late that afternoon. With our part of the signed contract in my briefcase we began a relaxed journey home. We had agreed a month to completion so that entry and removal arrangements could be made in an orderly way.

The following day when the Manchester solicitor discovered the property was already sold, his client made an enhanced offer to ours to release the property; but to no avail. Our clients were delighted with their purchase and nothing would have tempted them to sell for a profit.

For years now the house and its surrounding woodland have been not only their home, but also home to the birds, animals and all the creatures of nature which they have encouraged to live in peace and harmony with them.

Shortly afterwards I faced a similar challenge for an hotelier. On that occasion I used a similar action plan and I drove overnight to Wiltshire. I secured the property for him by exchanging contracts when the seller's solicitor opened his office at 8.30 the following morning.

My father's first advice when seated side by side in my Kentmere College was: "Get up early and get started in a morning." It has stood me in good stead!

So it was that my clients learned by practical experience the nature of a "contract race" when there is competition in a seller's market.

★   ★   ★

At Christmas we always had a jolly office party with a degree of leg-pull by staff and between the partners. My secretary/PA, Jean Cowling, sums up my shortcomings in her poem, If, with apologies to Rudyard Kipling.

# IF

## A Sixtieth Birthday Leg-pull by Jean Cowling
## 5th April, 2000 – Pip Pip!

**If** you can lose your files while all around are finding theirs
In places occupied by you;
**If** you can trust yourself when secretaries flout you
And make allowances for their sulking too;
**If** you can watch your weight although you're tired of dieting
And eat at Renoir's, meet with countless friends;
**If** you can drive a Jag, a bike and Penny Farthing
And know all about the geometry of bends;

**If** you've got a laptop that is hard to master,
**If** you can drink and still not spoil your aim;
**If** you can meet with Jean and Marilyn
And treat those two imposters just the same;
**If** you can rise at dawn and not be shirty,
Start dictating ere your legs have reached the floor
And often phone us up at seven thirty
To see what joys the diary holds in store;

**If** you can make one heap of all your earnings
And risk it all upon a new extension
That grows and grows but fulfils all your yearnings
With rooms and views that are all your own invention;
**If** you've got heart and nerve, when even in a tizzy,
To whom all turn when life is just a bummer,
And always want to know with what we're busy (!)
And buy ice creams for all of us in summer;

**If** you can talk in dialect, write verse and funny stories
That hold us all in sway;
**If** you like cows and selling cattle semen
And wonder where your in-tray is today;
**If** you can please the unforgiving Kendal
And fill your time sheets each and every one,
Yours is Hayton Winkley and all that's in it;
And, which is more, you'll be **LEN** my son.

Brow Top where I was born & Pumple Syke which we built new as our family home in Kentmere

Kentmere Tarn & view looking north into the Valley

Annie Mawson & her Celtic harp

Len's Windermere Grammar School
cap, Wetherlam House

Christine
Denmead,
book
illustrator
& friend

Sandra with our children Peter, Penny, Martin, Jacqueline, Ingrid & Nicholas & our golden retriever Amber plus my mother Evelyn Hayton's dog, Cammy in the garden at Pumple Syke, Kentmere

A CENTURY OLD FLYER! LH & Reg Gifford on sponsored Penny Farthing ride from Traveller's Rest, Grasmere to the White Lion in Ambleside. Picture taken at Pelter Bridge, Rydal (1986)

The head of Kentmere Valley from Brockstones Farm

# ISLAY CALLING

Picture of Portnahaven with arrow pointing to the cottage, our holiday home for 25 years

Left: Martin and Sandra at Saligo Bay on Islay

Sandra and Peter outside the cottage at Portnahaven, Islay

Sandra at Saligo Bay on Islay

# THE DAWN CHORUS

**1**

It's a-funny spot is this old world
But wat a grand spot t' be
When t' throstle sings his heart oot
On top of t'auld yak tree
An t' blackie up on t' lectric powl
Sticks oot his chest an sings
Just t' fetch anudder day
As t' birds aw stritch their wings

Ah stood theer in me neet clea's
Cos t' mworn was warm an still
An ah listened till aw oor fedthered friends
Up on't wooded hill
Ther was t' scoppie an't warbler an't pidgin
An't craw an laal wee chitty wren
An't cheeky sparra up on't spoot
Was chitteren noo an agean

**2**

Ah wakkened up just tuther mworn
Twas just aboot quarter t' fower
Ah gat mesel scraffeled oot o bed
An stood at oor back dooer
Ah listened wid simple thankfulness
T'dawn chorus was in full song
An ah'l tell yer this there's neea composer
Can match that merry throng

They war aw that thrang steakan ther claim
Till a bit o' t' countryside
An ivvery bird, beath big an smaw
Was singen far an wide
Ah wunder why th'aw start t' sing
When t' darkness starts t' wane
Its nobbut for hawf an oor er seea
Than aw ga's quiet agean

Ah thowt t' mesel hoo lucky ah was
T' stan an listen thear
Cos sum fwok travel's far an wide
But nivver t'dawn chorus hear
Yer can keep yer sunny Majorca
An yer villa oot in Spain
Just give me aw them fedthered friends
An ther chorus agean an agean

**Tommy Coulthard**



*The Dawn Chorus* by Tommy Coulthard with artwork by Robbie Ellis of Penrith

LH off on his morning bicycle ride *c.* 1995

Joy at Helme Lodge in Kendal *c.* 1995

Joy & LH at Levens Hall after her cancer diagnosis in July 2007. Joy died on 23rd December 2007

Mike & Kate who gave me much support on holiday with me in Scotland in 2009. Picture taken in Inverewe Gardens. Michael died in January 2010

# "Brightly dawned our wedding day!"

The collage of our Christmas card 2010. See *The Magic of the Internet*.

LH & Jean in MG approaching the Heaves Hotel for our wedding reception

My eldest daughter Jacqueline arriving with Millie & Jennie at Levens Church for our wedding in July 2010. Jackie died on 10th April 2016

View towards Grandy Barn in Kentmere where Jackie lived with her husband Gordon and family and is now laid to rest in Kentmere churchyard.

LH with his three best men (the Chums) & their wives before the wedding service: Jen & Bill Bewley; Peter & Joan Matthews; Tony & Jen Sansom

LH's PRIDE & JOY: MG TF 1954: purchased on 5th April 1983 & sold in September 2015 when no longer able to drive it

# LIFE ON TWO WHEELS WITH ROARING COMBUST!

LH & his 1928 Sunbeam motorbike at the 2002 Manx Rally on the Isle of Man

Jean after her first ride on the Moto Guzzi (2010)

Bill Bewley & LH at Lakeland Motor Museum with the Sunbeam motorbike beautifully restored by Bill (2016)

LH with his Moto Guzzi at the top of Kirkstone Pass (2008)

*Glorious Gardens from Above* LH being interviewed by gardening expert & presenter Christine Walkden at Levens Hall for the BBC series in September 2014

A day out & a much loved view of Wastwater

LH & Jean on their 6th wedding anniversary – a joyful day, July 23rd 2016 spent at the Fat Lamb Country Inn in Ravenstonedale. It has excellent facilities for the disabled

LH on mobility scooter with Jean & Andrew & Rona Bromley on our anniversary. Andrew was my law partner for 32 years

MISSING FROM THE LAKE DISTRICT! But where would you put a cable car? Aren't the elderly & disabled entitled to a view from a fell top?

When Michael Winkley retired in 2000, we started the new Windermere practice of Hayton Winkley Bromley Wood.

Andrew Bromley, Patricia Sanderson, LH and Keith Wood, partners in the Windermere firm of HWBW (2000) with our visiting ex-partner, Judge J. Anthony James in my garden at Quarry Foot, Levens

# CRISIS AT CHRISTMAS
## "This injunction threat could put me out of business!" said Smiley

Some years ago Smiley Distributor rushed into my office twelve hours before we were due to close for the Christmas holidays. He had received a High Court Writ claiming damages and an injunction for breach of the copyright/ patent in a design. I had to sit up and take notice, Christmas or no Christmas. There was a short time limit to enter an appearance to the Writ. The Plaintiff was a large national corporation with considerable resources and legal clout. There was no time to waste.

Smiley owned a number of wholesale and distribution companies in different parts of the country. They held large stocks of machinery spares for equipment used in the construction and transport industries. The value of the stocks ran into huge figures. Most of the stock was manufactured by

Stubborn Strongwill's company. His manufacturing company was the first Defendant named in the Writ. Smiley's companies, as distributors, were the second Defendants.

"Elizabeth, by the grace of God, we command you." These peremptory words, which prefaced the Writ of summons in those days, struck fear in many a defendant.

The Writ claimed an injunction against all the companies to cease manufacturing the spares and to stop distributing them or selling them at once. The Writ also claimed substantial damages. It would be a serious blow to Smiley if the Plaintiff were to succeed in putting a stop to his sales. It would put Smiley out of business and how would he avoid losing the value of his stock? Nevertheless, it seemed to me that Smiley was rather easy-going about it.

"Just thought, Len, I should pass this in front of you. I've talked to Stub Strongwill. He is the managing director of my suppliers and he says there is nothing in this; not to worry. He says I have to send him the Writ and he'll deal with it. What do you think? Stub has been a good friend and reliable supplier for years."

I enquired as to the background and read through the particulars of the claim. The allegation was that Strongwill's company was manufacturing the equipment in breach of the copyright and patents which the Plaintiff owned. The allegation, if true, was serious.

"But Stub say's there's nothing in it and he can prove it. It's his problem and I don't want to get involved with lawyers and legal fees."

I probed the facts a bit longer and felt very uneasy about Smiley's easy-going attitude and his faith in Stub. I could see a real conflict of interest if things went wrong and we did not have the facts.

Copyright and patent cases arise only occasionally in country practice and one cannot be an expert on every area of law. However, this is where the benefit of the two branches of the legal profession works to a client's advantage.

Solicitors in general practice are like doctors in general practice. They are able to examine the facts, diagnose the problem and have access to specialists with particular expertise. I immediately rang my London agent, a solicitor and friend of long standing. I asked him to recommend a firm with the best expertise in copyright and patent law. This turned out to be not only excellent advice but involved an amazing coincidence, as you will learn.

While Smiley nodded approval, I discussed the outline of the problem with the expert London solicitor and got a recommendation from him as to the most able barrister specialising in copyright litigation. I rang the specialist barrister's clerk and retained him. I confirmed the retainer in writing and sent him a copy of the Writ in that evening's post. There were no emails or fax machines then.

Smiley still wanted to let Strongwill deal with it himself in order to avoid legal fees. It emerged that Strongwill had employed a designer from the Plaintiff's company. My antennae were quivering now. I did not like the sound of that.

I advised Smiley that his own company was in direct line of fire. If his supplier was to take on Smiley's defence, I recommended that at the very least he should get an indemnity from the manufacturing company and an agreement to take back the stock at cost if his supplier lost the case. In the event that they failed in defending the action, the indemnity needed to cover Smiley against damages, losses and costs, if that could be negotiated.

Despite my advice Smiley still seemed happy to put his trust in Stubborn Strongwill. I was concerned. I had seen friendships dissolve so often where conflicts of interest arise. It is especially so when it comes to money and one's livelihood.

"At least," I said, "let us arrange a meeting with Stub Strongwill and get to know what has been happening." After some reluctance Smiley agreed to arrange a meeting shortly after Christmas. We agreed that I would travel with him to the manufacturing company's headquarters. We still had time to enter an appearance to the Writ to prevent judgement being entered. We had retained an expert barrister. Christmas carols were being sung and the coloured lights flickering in the street below reminded us it was Christmas.

Smiley clearly intended to enjoy Christmas. He had an instinct for self-preservation which had brought him to me, yet outwardly he preferred to be the cheerful optimist. "Come for a drink, Len," he said. "A new day and a New Year are coming. Have a drink, Len, and stop worrying!" Christmas came and went. We then made an early morning start to see Stub and his co-directors.

We were ushered into an oak-panelled board room by a very shapely personal assistant: a lovely greeting if ever there was one! Belinda showed us to our seats.

There, sitting foursquare on oak captain's chairs around a vast, solid oak table were the board members of the manufacturing company. All smiled a half smile simultaneously and nodded as if programmed together. It was clearly a 'them and us' situation. That was my clear impression.

At the head of the table, commanding immediate attention, was the Managing Director, whom I took to be Stub Strongwill. His huge, muscular frame rose from his seat, hand outstretched in a gesture of half-greeting and half-reluctance. He had a large cranium, a thick, bull-like neck and he thrust his head forward with a determined expression. He stopped short of leaning forward to shake hands. The half-gesture was all we deserved.

I got the impression he did not like solicitors and particularly one who was not prepared to do as he was told. He was used to being the boss.

I smiled, thanked him for his welcome and came to the point: "Can you tell us the background to this claim? I understand one of your designers once worked for the Plaintiff Company. It would help if I could get the feel of the matter."

"This is a b......waste of time. Thou just let me have Smiley's Writ and we'll deal with it," said Stub.

"But what happens if they win and Smiley can't sell his stock?" I asked.

"That will not happen. There is nothing in their claim. They won't win. Smiley is in no danger and neither is his stock," he said.

"Sorry, I am just a simple country solicitor and as I see it they have issued a Writ against Smiley also. He has to defend that Writ. You have the facts. If you want to handle the case you will need to make us aware of the background." I repeated my observation. "I believe you employ a designer who was previously employed by the Plaintiff. Has he anything to do with this claim?"

"Damn and blast, does thou think I am a fool? Our designs are original designs. He has designed our equipment with our design team. He assures me our design is original. There is no basis for their allegation that he has used his knowledge of their designs to help us.

"I have given him a reet grilling and I am satisfied he is straight; so thou hand over that Writ and git thysel back to Windermere! Thou wants to stick to a country solicitor's work. Thou knows nowt about copyright or patents law."

I could see no employee of his would dare to admit to Stub Strongwill that he was wrong or had been influenced by someone else's design. His insult stung me. I was familiar with the main principles of that field of law but was no expert. I knew enough to protect my Client.

I replied, "I know enough to realise that if there is substance in the detail of this claim that you are facing a real fight. They allege you have copied their design. I'm not going anywhere until I know what has gone on in your design department. If you are so sure of your case, then it is no skin off your nose to give Smiley an indemnity. There could be a hefty claim and it could put you and Smiley out of business. We have to put in an appearance to this Writ and prepare our defence."

"Thou's not gitten any indemnity from me! There's no need for any indemnity. We'll look after Smiley. He's been our customer for years. We look after our customers. There's no need for any indemnity. There is nothing in their claim."

"Well then," I said, "If there is nothing in their claim, there is no harm in giving the indemnity. You are not taking any risk in signing my indemnity if you are sure you are right. As it happens I have prepared an agreement for you to sign. If you want to conduct the whole case and Smiley's defence, then the simplest thing is to sign it. I have a copy of it here. It might be wise to ask your solicitor to look at it first."

"I want no solicitor," said Stub. "I know what an indemnity is. It means I cover the costs and any of Smiley's losses."

I handed it down the table. Stub's face was purple and all eyes were on him. I thought he would explode.

Smiley's face, coloured by years of his favourite whisky, was tense but the makings of a smug smile played around his mouth. He winked at me which I took to be encouragement. He was beginning to see my point. Stub saw the wink. An ugly scowl spread across his face but he spluttered, bit his lip and said nothing. He picked up my draft agreement and began to read.

There was a long silence while Stub read the indemnity.

I broke the silence. "As you will see, all we are saying is that in consideration of our releasing the conduct of Smiley's defence into your care, your company agrees:-

a) To conduct the defence professionally and supply us with copies of all pleadings and documents and correspondence as the case proceeds, so that we may comment if necessary.

b) To take back the stock at cost if they win.

c) To pay all legal costs of both Writs and to cover my firm's costs.

d) To cover the cost of any award for damages against Smiley or his companies.

e) Smiley will not claim damages for loss of profit against your company if you lose but will be happy if you pay for the stock. You will appreciate that if they win..."

"They are not going to b...... well win," exploded Stub. "They have no case and we have got a good team to work for us but for your damned interference."

"What do you mean my damned interference?" My hackles were beginning to rise. Smiley was grinning and he seemed to be enjoying the exchanges.

Stub Strongwill exploded and swore at Smiley, accusing him of grinning, winking at me and interfering. I then saw the blood rising up Smiley's neck like the neck of a turkey jock in a mating display. Smiley suddenly realised Stub could turn on him. He saw at last the importance of my advice: the need for the indemnity. He could see it very clearly now.

Smiley addressed Strongwill: "If they have no case Stub, why are you so reluctant to sign? It's a simple agreement. I am not asking you to cover more than the return of stock and the legal costs. You have all the facts. You know your designer man. I'm in your hands."

Stub went ballistic, cursing and swearing. Even his docile board, who until then had watched in silence, began to gesticulate for him to calm down.

"This bugger here," said Stub pointing at me, "has put a retainer on our man. Our London solicitor says we should have our usual top copyright barrister man, and this upstart solicitor from the backwoods at Windermere has put a retainer on our top man. Damn your hide!" he exclaimed, glaring angrily at me.

I looked at Smiley. His anger had subsided. He was grinning from ear to ear. He realised at last that we had given him the right Christmas present. When I had secured the retainer on the specialist Patent and Copyright barrister, I had by sheer coincidence engaged Stub's usual adviser and by chance had got in first.

"Give me a pen, Belinda!" Stub addressed his order to the shapely personal assistant who had ushered us in. She sat at a side table, dutifully taking notes during the meeting. Her face glowed. It was rare that anyone got the better of Stubby Strongwill and she couldn't help enjoying the moment, but in a protective sort of way.

Stub signed his name to the agreement, holding his pen like an iron bar and striking the paper with an angry flourish.

Belinda stood beside Stubby and leaned over him as she witnessed his signature. Her long nylon-covered legs were topped by a neat mini skirt. Her presence seemed to calm and mellow him. Having made the decision, his anger dissipated. I noticed Belinda sway slightly against him. She certainly had a calming influence. She smiled at Smiley and the board and looking sheepishly at me, she added, "I'll just make a photocopy." The board members nodded their assent to Belinda without saying anything. None of them had contributed a word to the proceedings.

Each of them nodded farewell but said nothing as Smiley and I took our leave. Stub, having recovered his composure, smiled engagingly and came out of the board room with us. He shook our hands in a most gentlemanly fashion, assuring us all the time that the Plaintiff had no case.

"Safe journey home," he said as we parted company. I wondered if he meant it!

Thereafter the case dragged on with procedures and negotiations through the High Court for almost two years, while the parties to the dispute argued in pleadings and in correspondence. It became clear that the former employee of the Plaintiff Company, who had subsequently worked for Stub's company, had indeed used the knowledge he had gained with the Plaintiff in designing the components for Stub.

Finally, Stubborn Strongwill's company had to compromise. Thus Stub had to cover my Client and indemnify him. Much of Smiley's stock, affected by the disputed copyright design, had to be returned at Stub's expense.

Our emergency action at Christmas had been successful in the end. The Indemnity Agreement had proved its worth and had also given Smiley time to re-source materials and protect his own businesses.

I wondered what crisis would happen next Christmas!

# TOAST TO THE HOTEL AND CATERERS' ASSOCIATION

In 1984 I was requested by the Hotel and Caterers' Association to address them as guest speaker at their Annual Dinner. The dinner was followed by a form of "Westmorland Merry Neet" with music, songs, verses and stories. I was asked to be the Master of Ceremonies and to tell some tales. Tony Kelly, silversmith and humourist, and John Shaw from Provincial Insurance provided music and laughter, with Ron Bell from Staveley, a real shepherd and singing countryman, who sang Lakeland hunting and country songs

It is hard to be an hotelier
And catering is worse
But to entertain hoteliers
Is hell itself in verse.

You work from early morning
In a kitchen steaming hot
To produce a fattening breakfast
For your carefree holiday lot.

You cut their luncheon sandwiches
They're off walking for the day
However cheesed off you may feel
You must cheer them on their way.

Some friendly folk come year by year
Like relatives they've become
And expect those little extras:
A night cap, hot milk with rum.

While nouveau riche in flashy car
Blonde concubine in tow
Has come to stay the weekend
Wild oats he intends to sow.

On high stools in the cocktail bar
Attired in the latest vogue
What affectation he takes on
To conceal the scheming rogue.

"Book it to my room, good man
We'll have a ball tonight
This malt must be Glenfiddich
The Pink Lady tastes just right!"

When morning comes there is no sign
Of scheming rogue and concubine
They drank your wine and ate their fill
Used your bed but paid no bill.

Alas the Porsche pushed silently away
Number changed by break of day
Sped off with your best warming pan,
Small antiques and copper can.

For other guests you still must smile
Egon Ronay here a while
Does he pay I often wonder
To criticise and cast asunder?

Now we live in the age of "Which"
Consumer guides have made their niche
Critics now for critics' sake
From their guides a fortune make.

On the Planning Board I often ponder
Direction signs they ban down yonder
Snakes and ladders their policy games
Finding hotels down country lanes.

Grants you get for bedrooms more
Tourist conditions by the score
What will you do when you're all five star?
Give a free night and a brand new car?

★   ★   ★

Back to the guests who fill your beds
Back to the drinkers who dizzy their heads
These are the folk who pay your bills
Coming to visit our Lakeland hills.
Back to the day-books now on the computer
The cash and the cheques from the tired commuter
Checking the till and counting the takings
Convincing the staff that "takings" aren't "makings".

When the accounts are done for the year gone by
The tax man will wonder: "Why oh why
Is the profit so modest there's no tax to pay?"
But you spend your whole winter in St Tropez!

★   ★   ★

Oh it's hell to be an hotelier
When the season's in full swing
But your success is our success
It's the business the tourists bring.

So we'll drink to the Hoteliers and Caterers
We'll now entertain you reet
With songs and tales and music
On this your Merry Neet!

***I give you the toast: "The Hotel and Caterers' Association"***

LH 01.02.1984

# MICHAEL WINKLEY'S 60th BIRTHDAY TRIBUTE

My partner, Michael Winkley, decided to retire from the firm as a partner in 2000 when he reached 60 but remain for a while as consultant at Kendal. Our Kendal partners, Peter, John and Naomi decided at that time that they wanted to steer their own ship and so we agreed on a demerger to take place the following spring. Thus my 35 years practising in partnership with Michael came to an end.

Kate, Michael's family and friends organised an evening at Kendal Golf Club to celebrate Michael's 60th birthday to which my late wife Joy and I were invited. Kate asked us to do a verse to Mike.

With the loss of Michael from a brain tumour in 2010, the memory of Mike's happiness that evening is the more poignant. It also gives a flavour of the man who was my friend for 52 years and my law partner for 35 years.

LH as Best Man to Mike at his Wedding to Kate

## 60th BIRTHDAY TRIBUTE
### *Saturday 2nd December 2000*
### *at Kendal Golf Club*

Ladies and Gentlemen:

I declare that this is a ***Without Prejudice Meeting*** which means you cannot use what I say in evidence!

Everything is ***Subject to contract***: which means you cannot bind me to it!

I give ***No Indemnities, Warranties or Guarantees***: which means I won't be responsible for what Joy or I may say about Michael!

It is on a ***Volenti non fit injuria*** basis: which means Mike & Kate asked us here so they are deemed to have given consent to whatever we might say!

CONFESSION:

But it is ***without prejudice also,*** because I have a confession to make to you all, the good people of Kendal and South Lakeland:

I carry a heavy responsibility, because I invited Mike to Kentmere in 1958

I invited him to join me in partnership in our Kendal office in October 1965

SO WE CELEBRATE TONIGHT not only his 60th Birthday but also our 35 years in partnership

Ladies and Gentlemen:

THOUGH I carry this heavy responsibility, for it is my fault that MSW came to Kendal, I know that he has ***always been the best and most reliable Law Partner I could possibly have had.***

He is a true professional – He always puts ***the interest of his Client first*** – sometimes to the annoyance of his partners, his family and even his golf pals. He is the epitome of a good family Solicitor as solicitors should be.

He ***is reliable and loyal,*** he works like an ox and he has ***resources of energy*** which frankly amaze me. Mike has done ***a great deal of good work in the town***. He has also provided lots of laughter, fun and goodwill amongst all his friends and acquaintances. I made an excellent move when I took him into partnership 35 years ago –

**<u>Aside</u>** – I could fill many verses with anecdotes of Mike's visits to Kentmere and our fun going to Blackpool in my old car but it would take all night. Michael used to love coming to Kentmere then. He loved to drive the tractors on our farm and he would turn hay then scale it – back and forth across the meadows. He was "cab happy" as we called it. His capacity for physical work and his energy seemed infinite.

When we were digging the hole for the septic tank for my parents' retirement bungalow in Kentmere in 1959, it was getting a bit deep for me to throw the earth out. Mike was taller (6 feet 4 inches), so he dug and dug all day until his head was level with the surface. A neighbouring farmer had watched this and enquired of my brother, "Who's gurt Irish navvy thou's gitten diggen that hoo-al? By God, he can dig!"

My father always said you could recognise a real friend by whether he would get his jacket off and help you when you were working. Mike did that and has proved to be a fine and reliable friend!

Mike, Reg Ashworth and I met at Blackpool Tech in 1958 to study for the Law Society's Intermediate Exam.

Our Law Faculty was situated on the same floor of the building as the Art College. We used to see the life models going to the life drawing classes and we were all rather curious to have a look at what went on! Mike in particular! This brings me to the poem I wrote for the office Christmas Party one year.

In the days before office parties were spoiled by noisy discos, we used to hold ours at the Blue Bell at Heversham, when it was in its prime. We dined on the best of John Chew's cuisine with the best hospitality one could wish for. Mike and I used to tell stories. That is where he began as a raconteur. To begin with it was his custom to recite Stanley Holloway's *Albert & the Lion*.

Staff took bets on how many verses he would remember! So for tonight I decided to do a sort of Stanley Holloway monologue for Mike and tell you about a prank we got up to when we were students at Blackpool Tech.

LH, Mike and Reg Ashworth on our 50th anniversary visit to Blackpool Law College, 15th September 2008

# MICHAEL AND THE MODEL

*With apologies to Stanley Holloway!*

There's a grand seaside place called Morecambe
That's renowned for Eric Morecambe and fun
It was there that the large Michael Winkley
Grew up and his law studies begun.

Now this is an un-authorised version
But authentic! – That mean's it is true
So we'll take the lid off young Winkley
And examine his sixty years through.

Well he was born a big baby to Nora
Of his masculine gender Alf Winkley was proud
And Michael grew up, well, fairly handsome
Because he stands quite high in a crowd!

And there's another seaside place – it's called Blackpool
Which is renowned for bonny girls and fun
It was there that I first met big Michael
At the law course where our studies begun.

Well, I was shy, en nobbut a country lad
Not used to the ways of the world
But Michael was handsome and confident
As our days at college unfurled.

Our lecture rooms adjoined the Art College
The artists' models were simply divine
And our masculine sap was moved by this
That urge of the male sublime!

When life drawing was in progress a notice said
"No entry. Knock and wait."
So Mike moved the notice to another door
As our lecturer was arriving late!

We explained to our kindly lecturer
You see he was gullible and slow
We told him the artists had more light in our room
But he wasn't bothered to know.

So straight way the brave little fellow
Not showing one morsel of fear
Took the door by its polished brass handle
And strode purposely reet in theer!

Big Mike and all of us following
Pushed in through the open door
A lovely blonde model in her birthday suit
Lay languid on the polished floor.

Our lecturer was most as-ton-ished
He turned in confusion and ire
While I noticed the blonde was a true blonde
Before she pulled on her kim-ono attire!

Well Michael was very gentlemanly
He felt he must comfort the blonde
Because Nora had taught Mike about manners
He could not just run off or abscond!

He pulled off a masterly confusion
We all left held in high esteem
And the lecturer too was bemused by Mike
For his persuasion drew off the steam.

It was then that I thought that's the fellow
This Mike is an unusual man
And I'm a bit odd and eccentric
That's how our friendship began!

⋆   ⋆   ⋆

**A happy Toast to Mike's 60th Birthday and 35 years in Partnership followed**

LH 2.12.2000

Mike Winkley as a young man with my parents, Joseph and Evelyn Hayton (standing) and Uncle Jack and Aunty Agnes on holiday on the south coast of England

# WESTMORLAND COUNTY AGRICULTURAL SHOW

My late wife Joy and I were delighted when the Society elected me as Vice-President in 2005, followed by President in 2006.

**Background** – My work for the Westmorland County Agriculture Society began in 1989 with the task of co-ordinating the sale of the old Kendal show site, then through the saga of finding a new site, with the eventual move to Lane Farm at Crooklands, near Kendal. This brought Joy and me into contact with a wider circle of the farming community of South Lakeland. We found all the farming families and business people who are members and/or support the Society to be the salt of the earth, reliable, friendly and a delight to know.

The legal issues I worked on included charity matters and redrawing the constitution with the late Chris Lambert, Roger Read, and the present Chief Executive of the Society, Christine Knipe. I have seen the tremendous work done by the Management Committee and the Showfield Director, Stephen Procter, in establishing the show in its new location. Since then Christine and her team have continued to carry out the Society's evolution policy and made the show blossom.

With the establishment of the Country Fest at the end of May and the study courses the Society provides, there is an all year round service to the members and to our community. The work which goes on throughout the year into the preparation for the annual Westmorland County Agricultural Show has to be seen to be appreciated.

WCAS banner of Rural Links Farm Open
Day for schoolchildren

# COUNTY SHOW ADVERTS

These adverts were broadcast at different times during the day on Lakeland Radio over a fourteen day period coming up to the Show, and I had some amusing reactions to them! They originally started in 2004 and have been used in various versions every year since then.

**Greetings, Ladies and Gentlemen. Welcome to
County Show time!**

This year (2006) I'm honoured to be your President of the Show.
Joy and I welcome you and hope you'll all come to the Show.

★    ★    ★

**Version 1: When oor stock is fit fer market**
En the harvest gathered in
When oor food's safe fer winter
En there's fuel in oor bin.

Then cast off o yer troubles
Be free fre o yer care
Polish yer be-ats en gird up yer gallasses
En let's o gang ta t' County Show Fair!

So hark, hark, hark forrad,
Hark forrad, come, come away!
T' fourteenth of September
Is oor County Show Day!

So write in yer diaries
T' fourteenth is the date
Before you're diverted
Lest your plans are too late.

Noo we welcome oor visitors
Wha come fre far en near
Ta sample oor good takkins
Mak merry en good cheer.

Thur's o maks o' animals, bring yer young folks ta see
T' best breeds in t' country as thur can be
Thur's o maks o' yows en o maks o' cows
Horses en goats, pigs, poultry en sows.

Thur's gallopen horses, Women's Institute courses
Thur's o maks garn on en plenty ta see
If thou's keen on fresh me-at en t' best country fare
Well t' food hall's a must: we'll be see-en you there!

What, we've acres of Trade Stands wi goodies galore
Ta buy at t' Show means sae much more!
Ye'll find o them trantlements, ye've sought far en wide
Though tractors en implements fre t' wife thou can't hide!

But don't worry cos t' wife en t' children en o
Can find what they want at oor grand country show
En we've fancy boddies commen: celebrities I mun say
But I can't tell yer noo: you mun come on the Day!

---

**Version 2: Hark! Hark! Hark forrad! Hark forrad, let's away**
On t' fourteenth o' September it's County Show Day!
But it isn't just farming, thur's country pursuits
Business en commerce, pleated skirts en fine suits!

Ancient but modern I.T. courses we run
Fer all ages at all stages: we mak learning fun!
Oor Society is active throughout t' four seasons
A community dynamo fer many, many reasons.

Oor Rural Links Team holds Farm Open Days
When schoolchildren en students see best farming ways
Like oor founding pioneers two centuries ago
We promote best farming practice on oor farms and on t' Show.

But oor Show is t' flagship, oor 'raison d'être'
Thur's plenty ta do en ta see etcetera, etcetera
Fer o'er two hundred year folk hev com tul oor Show
Sick grand traditions we mon't let em go.

So remember, remember t' fourteenth of September
The Westmorland County Show
Relax, watch t' wrestling en o t' ring events,
O t' displays en crafts roond t' showfield in t' tents.

En young folks, please remember oor traditions lang sen
When coy country lasses wud wink at thur men
Thur'll be bonny lasses on horses; aye, lasses o roond
Wi young hansom fellows on t' County Show Groond!

★   ★   ★

So we're o' looken forrad ta see-en you at t' Show
It's turble good value as maist o' yer will know
En hev a good day oot!

Yer knaa t'ald folk used ta say:
"A good laugh en a good crack wi yer friends is worth o yer physic!"

August 2006

*Hark! Hark forrad! It's County Show Day!* It is a One Day Show attended by an average of 35,000 people. It is one of the best one day shows in the whole of the UK

# 4

## ISLAY CALLING

Our early visits to Scotland as a family had been by car and caravan to the Mull of Kintyre and the Isle of Arran. While staying on the Kintyre peninsula, we noticed a number of dwellings in ruins and we decided to advertise in the Oban Times for such a cottage, with a view to restoring it as a family holiday home over time.

After buying the cottage on Islay in Portnahaven, we purchased a second-hand Range Rover which was one of the first series with washable seats, not the luxury car of today. It had plenty of room for our six children and Amber, our golden retriever, plus all the panoply of family things.

At home on our smallholding in Kentmere, the Range Rover allowed us to cart hay-bales on a flat trailer and keep the children safe when travelling

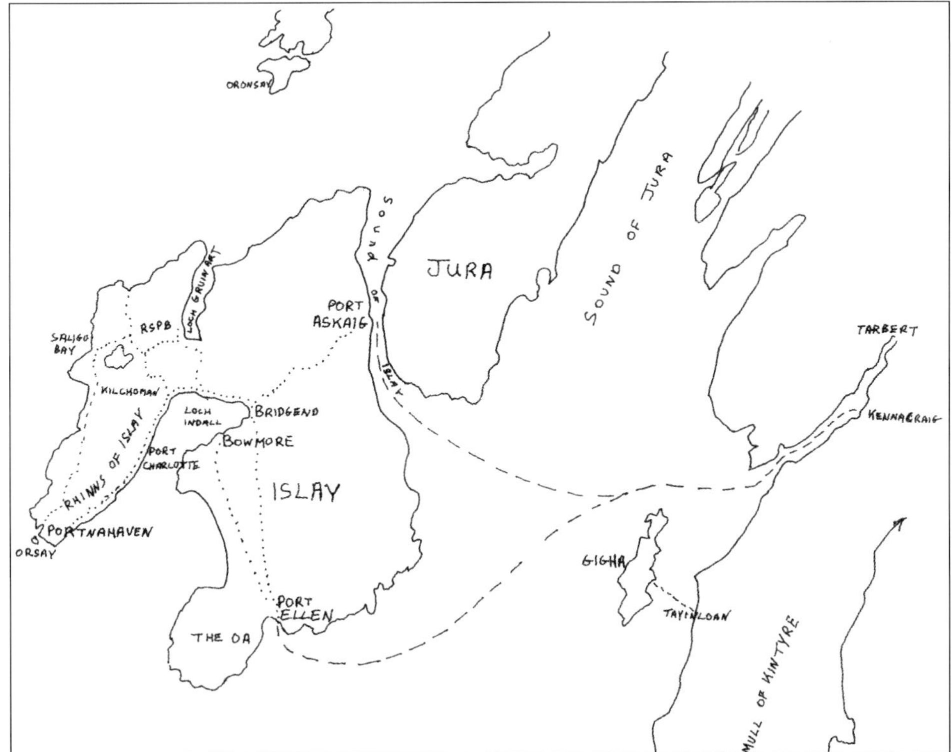


LH's sketch map of Islay

between the fields and our barn. On Islay where we had acquired a peat-cut high on the moor, the car proved ideal for bringing down the peats to our cottage. We had many an enjoyable day with the children cutting peat and then setting four pieces up on end like sheaves of corn so that they would dry, ready to be brought down to the cottage in time for our next visit in the autumn. I recall the smell of burning peat mixed with the sea air. It is a lovely memory. We owned the cottage in Portnahaven for approximately 25 years, selling it in 1997. See the pictures of our family on Islay in the colour section of this book.

# ISLAY – MY FIRST VISIT

"You're no going ta build the new Nessy there er ye?"

My first visit to Islay in the spring of 1970 was to view a cottage in the village of Portnahaven on the south end of the Rhinns of Islay, just 30 miles or so as the crow flies from the north of Northern Ireland. Islay is the most southerly island of the Inner Hebrides.It is a two and a half hours' sail west from Kennacraig on the Mull of Kintyre.

★　★　★

"You're no going ta build the new Nessy there er ye?" We stood up from our measuring. The question had come from a pear-shaped, apron-clad old lady, standing on Queen Street above us, looking down like a rather genial emperor-penguin with her white apron.

The back garden, or more precisely the wilderness, at 10 Shore Street in Portnahaven on the island of Islay, dropped steeply from Queen Street above, from where Bella McEwan was watching us, down to the cottage in Shore Street which we were proposing to buy. The view south over the old abandoned fishing port out across the open sea to the lighthouse on Orsay Island was breathtaking.

"Are you from the Bureau? "Bella asked. "I hear we're having a new Nessy in Portnahaven. I hope you're not going to build it there." She had mistaken us for officials from Argyll County Council. I discovered later that the existing Nessy (community toilet) stood roofless on the shore, still in use, but mainly as a shelter from the wind to consume whisky after the pub had shut! The empty bottles round the pan told their own story. See the poem: *This Thing We All Need.*

My companion and I had been measuring the boundaries of 10 Shore Street which included a long strip of steep ground rising directly to the front of the McEwan's house in the street above. Bella was greatly relieved when I told her that I had advertised in the Oban Times for a holiday cottage needing repair. An Englishman in the south of England had responded, sending a postcard of Portnahaven with the cottage arrowed, together with a very large key for the mortice lock on the front door. The postcard and key were so intriguing that I had decided that the two and a half hour trip by sea from West Loch Tarbert on the Mull of Kintyre would be part of a real adventure. So it was that I found myself meeting Bella and her husband, both then well into their eighties. They were the first of many warm and friendly folk we grew to respect and love on this beautiful Hebridean island.

Bella was greatly relieved that we were not measuring up for the "Nessy" and invited us to afternoon tea: "When you have finished your surveying." Her soft Gaelic accent was warm and melodic .We accepted at once and a little while later she reappeared in her Sunday apron and announced that tea was ready. It turned out to be Grandad McEwan's birthday tea!

The table was laden with scones, jam and cakes. Beside our place mats stood a pint glass of beer and the largest dram of pure malt whisky that I had ever seen. It was an evening of stories, good humour, drams and genuine Islay hospitality.  Finally with the warm, cosy feeling that is peculiar to good Gaelic company and Islay malt, we persuaded them to let us go and find some accommodation.

"Och Len–art! There's nowhere in Portnahaven ye can find a bed and breakfast the noo. Number 10 Shore Street will be damp and there's nay beds. We'll hev ta see if we can persuade Maureen McKinnon at the pub ta give ye a room. We hevna a spare room the neet, for our daughter Wendy is commen!"

It was very late but Bella used all her charm and arranged for Maureen to give us a room. There were not many tourists on Islay at that time. It was a sparsely furnished room but it had the most wonderful, uninterrupted view of the lighthouse and the ocean. We went to sleep that night listening to the roar of the mountainous waves boring through between the islands at the mouth of the harbour inlet.

It was the first of many nights I would spend on the beautiful island of Islay where the lighthouse flashed its beam on seals basking only a few feet from us and illuminated our bedroom walls as we slept. So it was that thirty years of lasting friendships were formed on Islay.

Bella and her husband have long since been laid to rest in the windswept cemetery on the Rhinns of Islay facing the sea they loved. Over the years we took part in evenings of singing and live accordion and bagpipe music at various celebrations and ceilidhs. Days were spent talking and walking the cliffs and shoreline with family and friends.

Although we were holiday visitors, the Rhinns folk seemed more hospitable than most. Many of the Islay folk and their children had to spend their

Bowmore is the capital of the island. From the harbour you can see the famous round church – so the devil can't hide in the corners!

working lives at sea or over on the mainland and were used to folks coming and going away for long periods. They would say when we returned to the cottage: "Och Len-art, you've come home then!" We entered into the fun and enjoyed real Islay ceilidhs which seemed to us a mix between a Lakeland Merry Neet and a Highland Romp!

But one story of a ceilidh still tickles me concerning the McEwans. It was following a ceilidh in the Rhinns Hall at Portnahaven. It had been a night of dancing, highland flings, songs and stories. The kilts and the lassies had been swinging to the wild antics of the Islay men! The bagpipes, the accordions, the fiddles and the songsters had all played their part – young and old. What a night! Afterwards it was the practice for the islanders to return with friends to their homes where they would continue their enjoyment in songs and stories. Of course there were more of the drams of whisky. We were invited back too. It was just such a night which prompted me to embellish a true story told to me by Wendy, the Mc Ewans' daughter, of what occurred at their home after a ceilidh.

There was a glowing peat fire which lit up the bare boards and floor joists of the bedroom above. Grandpa McEwan went to bed. Meanwhile Gilbert, who was I believe a relative, lay snoozing on the hearthrug below. Everybody seemed to be related to each other in some way on Islay.

I have taken some poetic licence and embellished the story a little in my poem *After a Ceilidh on Islay*.

# AFTER A CEILIDH ON ISLAY

★   ★   ★

'Twas after a ceilidh on Islay,
The folks came home for a chat.
There was drinking and singing in Gaelic,
As round the peat fire we sat.

Grandad was tipsy,
So he went to bed.
His bedroom was sited
Just over our head.

Poor Gilbert McWhatsit
Was having a snooze,
Half paralytic
On whisky and booze.

He lay on the hearthrug
Full length on his back,
Directly beneath
A bedroom floor crack.

Grandad upstairs
Undressed to his skin,
Searched under the bed
For the pot to piss in.

Unsteady, unstable,
He slowly took aim,
But whatever he tried,
The result was the same.

For Grandad was bursting
On drams and whatnot,
And his sight was impaired
For locating the pot.

While some found its target
A great deal went by,
And ran through the crack
Where Gilbert did lie.

Now Gilbert was dreaming
Of a land fresh and fair,
Where the drink was all free,
And the girls were all bare.

He lay in the shade
Of a coconut tree,
And dreamt that the nuts
Were full of whisky.

The sun through the fronds
Seemed to glint on the juice,
As a crack in the coconut
Let the whisky come loose.

Gilbert drank of the nectar
Tasty and sweet,
For it came clean through Grandad
Pure and neat!

# ISLAY

Dreams, Drams, Birds, Sea and Silver Sands

## ISLAY CALLING

### *SONG*

I climbed in my motor early one morning
The sun it was rising above the blue sea
I boarded the ferry and sailed for the Island
That has such sweet memories for all friends and me.

Headed west bound for Islay and sailed south of Jura
Up through the sound to the Port Askaig quay
I saw that fine Island that lay sheened in sunlight
An Island of beauty, so lovely to see.

I've wandered the rocks around Portnahaven,
I've sat on the quayside and pondered awhile
I've sat among seabirds, watched the flight of the fulmar
And laughed with your people, seen their friendly smile.

But never, oh never, have I ever, ever
Experienced such peace or friendship so true
Your welcome, your whisky, the joy of a ceilidh
Just the happy experience of being with you.

I'm so tired of the rat race, I'm sick of the system
I'm going back to Islay, that gem in the sea
For your life is the real life, a life that's worth living
Our lives are God-given: we must spend them free!

These words I wrote for Peter McArthur of Portnahaven who sang them to an old Gaelic refrain. He used to entertain us with his lovely tenor voice at the ceilidhs and in his home. Peter also sang Scottish and Celtic songs, sometimes with gusto and at other times to haunting melodies with Gaelic words, which always had to be translated for us. Peter and his mother Naari always made us welcome, like mariners home from the sea.

Robbie Ellis recorded and sang this beautifully on my CD: *Tales of a Lakeland Lad*. You can hear it by logging on to Robbie's website which is illustrated in this book.

# ODE TO SANDRA ON SALIGO BAY ISLAY

## In the moonlight

Lady moon her soft light shining
Through the wisps of cloud on high
Spreads her moonbeams on the water
Over sand dunes where we lie.

Across the arc of silver seashore
Clean sand glistens in the light
Before my eyes a scene of beauty
Resplendent on this perfect night.

Great rollers gallop to the shoreline
Crested by their silver mane
Rise in splendour, phosphorescent
Break, then fall away to roll again.

Beyond the bay a jagged headland
Inky black in silhouette
Prescribes by rock the ocean's limit
Eternal granite solid set.

The sweep of sky a dome above us
Studded stars in bright array
Timeless patterns gems suspended
All along the Milky Way.

Not a sound except your breathing
Save distant lapping of the tide
You my love, asleep and dreaming
Serene and happy by my side.

Lady moon's soft light caressing
Through the ringlets of your hair
Touches lips, highlights your beauty
You, my angel, lying there.

LH Islay 20.08.1980

# THIS *THING* WE ALL NEED

The "thing we all need" which inspired this verse was situated down on the seashore at Portnahaven on Islay. It had walls and a door but the roof had blown away in the gales. At night the only illumination was from the moon or the intermittent beam of the lighthouse on the little island of Orsay. Before we installed a toilet in our cottage, we had to use this basic facility! I shall always recall it being uniquely in tune with the natural world around me, as I listened to the cries of the seabirds and the waves lapping on the shore. I could hear seals on the rocks close by.

The Norse men (Vikings) also  stayed at Loch Finlaggan on Islay around 850 to 1200AD. They also had a "thing" – it was a meeting place or parliament – as in the case of the Tynwald on the Isle of Man. For my part, the "thing we all need" is a place for thought and contemplation. For those of you good enough to purchase this book, the "thing we all need" is a good place for browsing! But of all the fine sedentary receptacles I have ever visited, this one is perhaps the most memorable!

★    ★    ★

Whatever one's station
Whatever one's creed
We all visit daily
This *thing* that we need.

Long before the Stone Age
When the wild woods would do
The spirit of nature
Was worshipped all through.

No disinfectant was needed
No pipes nor a flush
The tribe kept a look-out
For wild beasts in the bush.

When kings went to battle
It wasn't the royal throne
That they valued as much
As a receptacle two tone.

It was fashioned in oak
And gilded in gold
It was velvet and soft
In the brave days of old.

In youth in my valley
It was way up the yard
From a warm bed each morning
The journey was hard.

A large hole for Father
Was too big do you see?
So a second he made smaller
Especially for me!

We sat there together
And looked down the dale
While newspaper cuttings
Hung down from a nail.

Though this function we don't mention
There are euphemisms galore!
Where graffiti and carvings
Are all over the door.

Each home has its palace
Tiled right up the wall
With soft scents and tissues
And pot plants so tall.

But of all the fine palaces
And décor I've seen
There's none to compare
With one place I have been.

Where the sky was my ceiling
And the moon shone above
There I sat in the ruin
And heard seals making love.

The hinges were rusty
Where hung the old door
While waves were heard lapping
Nearby on the shore.

Sweeping the night sky
Was the lighthouse beam
Spotlighting my haven
With its far fleeting gleam.

Though the walls were all covered
With moss and green slime
And the sand blown all over
Was mingled with grime

The sea air was so bracing
I felt peaceful and free
My spirit soared like a fulmar
Sweeping over the sea.

And there on that island
Where the moon lit the shore
As I sat looking out
Through the old ruined door
I reflected:

Whatever one's station
Whatever one's creed
It's the one place we're all equal
On this "thing" we all need.

LH  20.7.1999

# COME HOME MY LOVE TO ME

## SONG

I wrote this song also for  Peter McArthur of Portnahaven who sang it to an old Gaelic melody. Robbie Ellis also recorded and sang this beautifully on my CD: *Tales of a Lakeland Lad.*

*Chorus:*
Drawn am I to the Rhinns of Islay
Fascinated by the sea
Spirit of my loved one calling
*Come home, my love, to me.*

★　　★　　★

On the wild and rugged headland
Where the rocks defy the sea
There my own sweet loved one perished
She was swept away from me.

I could only watch in anguish
Helpless I, a hapless boy
Taken by the hungry ocean
There I lost my pride and joy.

As she danced beside the water
Tempting waves on slippery rock
Back and forward like a plover
The mighty ocean she did mock.

Now she's gone, I'm left forever
Restless I like restless sea
But my heart remembers ever
Sparkling eyes that shone on me.

*Chorus:*

Drawn am I to the Rhinns of Islay
Fascinated by the sea
Spirit of my loved one calling
*Come home, my love, to me.*

LH 1975

# MY ISLAY MINCE

On one of our long weekend trips to Islay with Chums Bill, Tony and Peter, it was my turn to cook the evening meal. My speciality was a sort of cottage pie. Thus the four of us called in at Mrs Gibson's, the butcher's and general store in Bowmore, the main town on Islay, for provisions. Mrs Gibson had a lovely warm Hebridean accent.

While being barracked and teased by the Chums, much to Mrs Gibson's amusement, I asked for *one* piece of cheese, *five* carrots, *one* turnip, *six* potatoes, *two* onions, *six* shallots, *eight* rashers of bacon for breakfast the next day, *one* packet of beef stock and *one* of chicken.

I then asked for some mince for the cottage pie. Mrs Gibson looked rather quizzically at me and smiled warmly. In her lovely melodic voice she asked:

**"And hoo many strands of mince will you be wanting?"**

Chums and wives outside 10, Shore Street, Portahaven, Islay. From left: Jen Sansom, Peter Matthews, Jen Bewley, Tony Sansom, my late wife Joy, LH and Bill Bewley. Peter's wife, Joan, took the photo.

# BURNS NIGHT SUPPER SONG at the 41 Club

*Originally composed for Kendal Caledonian Society Luncheon*

## A TOAST

*Recalling Andy Stewart and Duncan Macrae at Hogmonay
singing "Campbelltown Loch I wish you were whisky"*

**"Len-art ma lad"**
(Me talking to myself and wishing I'd been born a Scot)


*Chorus:*
*Och Len-art ma lad, I wish ye were Scottish*
*Len-art ma lad, och aye!*
*Och Len-art ma lad, I wish ye were Scottish*
*And I'll tell ye the why.*


For I'd be born in a glen and they'd call me MacLen
Ma legs would be hairy and frisky
I'd enjoy a wee dram to set me off hame
And my blood would be warm with the whisky!


*Chorus*


Och if I was a Scot, it's as sure as it's not
That I'd be a man of brains
I could be a hob-nob with the very top job
Where the "Iron Chancellor" reigns.


*Chorus*


I could run at some pace, and grimace ma face
As I heave and toss the great caber
So with ma muscles in order I'd rove over the border
And harass my English neighbour.


*Chorus*


Och Len-art MacLen you could go now and then
To grave out your peats in lots
Or peacefully float in a bonny wee boat
And empty your lobster pots.


*Chorus*


I could go as of reet to a jolly Burns Neet
To the Haggis I'd write a wee ode
And return to ma sleeps full of whisky and neeps
Doon Tam'o Shanter's road.

*Chorus*

I could pipe secret peat-water to a still that I oughter
Not use without Customs' consent
But in a wee but–en-ben this naughty MacLen
Could make nectar one hundred per cent!

*Chorus*

I could tell a wee joke in this mack-o-talk
And sing with a highland lilt!
I could find a wee lassie: aye and make a wee passie
And show her what's under ma kilt!

*Chorus*

Like the late Duncan Macrae I'd enjoy Hogmanay
If I could recite *The Wee Cock Sparra*
If I happened to roam far away from ma home
I would take ma strang bow and ma arra!

*Chorus*

On this Bonny Burns Neet, och we'll no hev a fight
But we'll sing of Auld Lang Syne
We'll all join our hands with folks from far lands
And pray for World Peace in our time.

★   ★   ★

But I leave you with the thought:
Ma ancestors sailed here in a Viking lang-boat
With the Norse-blood rich in thur veins
To dwell in Strathclyde which stretched doon here from the Clyde.
After lang fights o'er the border, there is now law and order
And it's the Haggis and the Whisky that reigns!

Now let's toast you good Caledonians
May all of you be Aeonians:
That means everlasting, forever;
And no matter what; each be a good Scot
And don't lose your character – Never!

I give you the Toast:

TO OUR SCOTS FRIENDS!

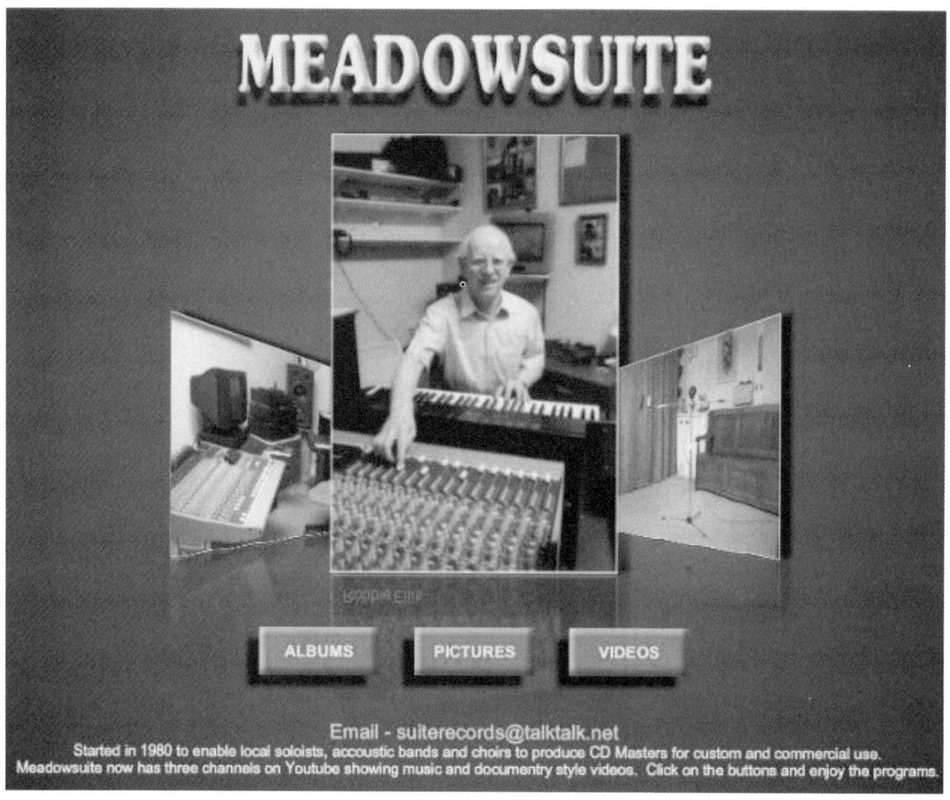


Robbie Ellis' website can be found at www.wix.com/meadowsuite/albums Also on Facebook – Robbie Jenny Ellis

*5*

―――

# MUSINGS & AMUSINGS

The following is a miscellaneous collection of whimsical and reflective pieces which I have written from time to time, as the spirit has moved me.

# "REAL LIVE NATIVES"

I recall an occasion at Ambleside over twenty years ago. I was with my good friend, Bill Bewley, chatting and having a quiet drink in the bar of the Waterhead Hotel at the head of Lake Windermere. Unknown to us an American lady, rather overdressed and bejewelled but full of enthusiasm, had been listening to our conversation.

We were talking about Bill's business and work. In those days he used to pull my leg and say that he was "just a poor boatman" but behind all the leg pull he has always been a loyal and inspiring friend to me and my family and a sound businessman of Lakeland.

The American lady interrupted our conversation as through the window we watched the large lake steamer called the "Swan" docking at Waterhead Pier.

***"Gee fellas, does the Queen Mary dock at this pier?"***

We looked up in amazement. Windermere is a lake, the biggest in England, 11 miles long, but the American lady had clearly not considered the implications.

The Teal, sister ship to the Swan, on Windermere

***"Say, do you come from these parts?"*** We nodded in agreement and explained that our ancestors had lived in Westmorland for centuries.Before we could say another word she shouted and waved her arms at her husband on the other side of the room.

***"Hey, Wilbur-Fred, baby! Come here Wilbur! Here's some real live natives!"***

# REAL LIVE NATIVES

Ya neet a lile bit sen
It was summer sort o' wedder
A local pal and I went oot
Ta hev a sup tagither.

We talked en joked, we laughed en smoked
As time went murrily by
When a Yankee woman powdered en permed
Cem exen us reasons why:

*Did the Queen Mary dock at Waterhead?*
*Where was this Roman camp?*
*She wanted some of this Lakeland rock;*
*Was England always wet and damp?*

*Did we really live in Lakeland?*
*Were we really born and bred?*
***"Say honey baby, come and see***
***Here are some real live natives! Wilbur-Fred!'***

Well Bill and I felt special then
And ever since that day
I've felt a real live empathy
With the red Indians down Wyoming way

I say to myself is this a reserve?
Are we country folk on display?
Or can we keep a balance,
Give pleasure, yet let them pay?

When a theatre's full they close the door
And no one parks in the aisle
If I barge into a performance
I'm not greeted with a smile.

Should the tourist pay an entrance fee*
Or visit our Lakeland free?
When I go to a town or a theatre
I buy a ticket; they charge me!

*An interesting thought prompted by the fact that when we entered Switzerland by road in 1979 we had to buy a *carnet* to put on the windscreen. It was a kind of toll for using the roads and tunnels which the Swiss had built and which were being used to shorten journeys by travellers from neighbouring countries through the Alps rather than go around them. It was clear that neighbouring users should contribute to the maintenance costs.

I have often thought our Government and planners could learn a great deal from the Swiss. They provide excellent facilities for tourists without spoiling the visual amenity. Visitors also get special travel passes to enhance their enjoyment in return.

We could use the tolls accumulated to improve our facilities for tourists – underground car parks – keep toilets open – a cable car – to support local trusts like the Armitt Library and grant-making trusts for apprenticeships!

★　★　★

# POKEN ABOOT AMANG PAPERS

They say *"the road to Hell is paved with good intentions."* Over the years I have occasionally found time to start tracing my ancestors, but I have not completed the branches of my family tree, so it cannot appear here. By the year 2000 I had traced the male line back to John Hayton, who had married Margaret Longstaff in 1702. I went looking for wills in the Archives at Carlisle. After looking at papers all afternoon, I wrote *Poken Aboot Amang Papers* the following morning.

## *PROLOGUE*
### Three Hundred Years of Haytons

**"Ald John"** begat Joseph in 1702, **Joseph** begat Joseph in 1739, **Joseph** begat Joseph in 1775, **Joseph** begat Gerard in 1809 (Reverend Gerard), **Reverend Gerard** begat Joseph in 1847, **Joseph** begat Gerard in 1870, **Gerard** begat

Joseph in 1895 and **Joseph** begat **my brother Gerard in 1929, my brother Jack in 1931 and Leonard – that's me – in 1940.**

### *A Visit ta Archives ta Find Ald John Hayton's Fadder!*

I was wanten ta knaa wha'd faddered **ald John**
Fer it seemed o oor records en papers hed gone
En whar were his parents, his sibbins, his wife?
Whar (where) did he leeve (live) en wat soo-art of life?

So off up ta Carrel (Carlisle) I med mi arn way
I was poken amang papers fer t'main of a day
T'Archivist lant up wid a turble ald Will
O' John Hayton and Family: did they leeve ut Gill?

T'Gill was a farmstead under Orton Fell
If t'farmhouse could talk, wat tales it might tell!
Mappen wad knaa wat happened ta ald John
Fer he nobbut married his Maggie in seventeen-o-one!

Maggie bore lile Joseph in seventeen-o-two
Thomas a bit later, wid a third commen through!
Then John on his deathbed left his Will-makken late
Because he deed three days later: that was 1708!

So on t'28th of October o' that seam eer
John left o his belongings ta them he held dear.
T'Will said: "Sick in his body but soond in his heead"
But three days later, he was liggen deead!

John left all his heirlooms ta his eldest lad, Joe
En thur's a second lad Thomas, the Will let's us know.
"To his loving wife Margaret and the child in her womb"
He left annual rents when he went ta his tomb.

As John was a tailor ut a gay fancy time
He wad likely mek folderals en fashions sae fine
That t'gentryfolk buyers wad pay him gay weel
En he'd mak a fair profit fre ivvery deal!

Ta his best friends and brothers he left hats, coats and rings
O his clay-uths en his brutches en his fine personal things
But what happened ta Margaret? I'se gay moidered ta knaa
What of t'barn she was carry-en? Did it fend? Did it graa?

Well John left forty pund if t'barn was a lass
But a lad wad git fifty – if that com ta pass!
So dootless relieved when t'barn was a lad
She caw'd him lile John, mebbe efter his Dad.

Well I hope that t'ald sayen proved reet in the end
That *"**A woman will thrive whar a man cannot fend**"*
But alas in t'ald records just twelve eer on
Maggie hed deed leeven Joe, Thomas en lile John.

Joseph survived because mi line he begat
En t' prologue records t'whole o' that
But I was gitten di-verted fre ald John's fadder
I needed ta find t'next step up t'ladder.

Well in t'sixteen hundreds thur's Haytons galore
O leeven roond Orton, but behint which doo-er?
Thur was an ald Thomas wha leeved at t'Gill
He hed a son John, but I'se wonderen still …

Poken aboot amang papers three hundred eer ald
Can git turble misleaden when t'evidence is cald
En yer heead gits o'er heated as puzzlement graas
Fer corroboration is elusive as I'se sure thou knaas!

So I'se still wanten ta knaa wha faddered ald John
I gat up a blind alley en mi time hed gone
*If I could nobbut find ald John's bayens (bones) up Orton way,*
**I'd call in them experts on D.N.A.!!!**

LH 26.09.2000

Notes. i) We have now established that John's father was named Lancelot and came from Asby – the next parish to Orton. We have also visited a place called Hayton Holme in the said parish, but we do not know if he lived there at the time of the Civil War. ii) We recently discovered that in the 1700s Haytons owned and farmed land in Bretherdale at a farm called Dog Lumb and at Beckside and Midwathstead. I can truly claim that I am a local lad because all my Hayton ancestors dating back to 1600 lived in Westmorland. There were also Hayton families living on the Shap Abbey Estate when the Abbey was dissolved by Henry VIII in 1540. iii) For dialect words please see Main Glossary.

# A CENTURY OLD FLYER
## "High above the ground"

Gliding happily along five feet from the ground
No chain wheels, no rattles nor mechanical sound
A fresh wind on my face and blowing through my hair
On that sunny spring morning I abandoned all care.

I observed from my perch there high above the ground
Cud-chewing cattle and sleepy sheep in fields all around
On that lovely fine morning, oh the birds they did sing
And church bells in the distance I could hear faintly ring.

Though precariously seated so far from the ground
My passage no longer obstructed by stones or a mound
I was thrilled by the freedom, the gliding, the grace
As over smooth modern tarmac I sped at gazelle-like pace.

I saw in the hedgerows from my perch above ground
The birds building nests in safe places they'd found
And into hedge bottoms the rabbits did scurry
As my ancient invention caused panic and flurry!

The spoon brake is useless, so an uphill must be found
To slow down my progress and alight on the ground;
Oh the thrill and elation feels truly extra-ordinary
When I glide through the lanes on my century-old "Ordinary"!

LH 17.11.1999

*A Century Old Flyer* recalls the delightful experience of riding my Penny Farthing or 'High Bicycle.' Sometimes I would take an early morning spin from Pumple Syke, our family home in Kentmere, to Millriggs or to Sawmill Cottage to visit Gordon Fox, the renowned Kentmere potter, and his wife Barbara. Sometimes I would sit with Gordon and Barbara and listen to him playing Chopin's *Nocturnes* and Mendelssohn's *Songs without Words* on his baby grand piano. He has a wide repertoire which includes jazz, and it was always a delight to hear him play.

LH riding past Ambleside market cross

The poem also reminds me of the ride with my friend, Reg Gifford, from Grasmere along Rydal Water to Ambleside on a beautiful morning with our friends. See the colour photo of the two of us dressed in Edwardian costume beside Pelter Bridge. I did a number of runs for charity over the years on my Penny Farthing. The photo on page 106 recalls an Ambleside event to raise money for the RNLI, and I recall gliding along through Ambleside on the early morning ride with no traffic to get in the way of progress!

# MY PENNY FARTHING
## Or High Bicycle or Ordinary

### *Historical notes*

The Penny Farthing was first invented in 1871. It was a development from the earlier 'Velocipede' or 'Boneshaker'. As early as 1819/1820 a London coachbuilder had invented a 'Pedestrian Accelerator' which was a type of hobby horse with two wheels and a seat between, astride of which the rider ran and no doubt rode between bouts of running or downhill travel.

The Penny Farthing was originally called the 'High Bicycle' or the 'Ordinary' because it was the ordinary bicycle of its day before the safety bicycle was invented in 1885. Penny Farthings were very popular in the 1870s and 1880s, and during that period 250,000 were made. Bicycle clubs sprang up and races were held, attended by large numbers of people. H.L.Cortis was the first man to cover twenty miles in one hour on a High Bicycle. It is reported that travelling one hundred miles in a day on a Penny Farthing became commonplace, even on the road surfaces of that time. The biggest problem then, as today, when riding a Penny Farthing is the 'header' or 'imperial crowner' when you go over the handlebars if your passage is suddenly obstructed! Fortunately I have never done so.

It was in Kentmere where I first saw a Penny Farthing. It belonged to my friend Martyn's mother, Jane Wrathall. The Wrathalls had an antique shop in Kendal. Their home was Capplerigg, which had been the Kentmere Church vicarage, built when my great great grandfather was the Parson. We learned to ride the Penny Farthing in Kentmere.

The radius of the Penny Farthing's

"Doing a Header!" The Knutsford Great Race Programme 2010

LH as the Mad Hatter, 1955

LH on Penny Farthing at Pumple Syke

large front wheel should normally equate to the length of the cyclist's inside leg measurement. The wheel on the Wrathall's bicycle was much smaller than the bicycle I later owned and this enabled me as a teenager to ride it comfortably. On the occasion of Speech Day at Windermere Grammar School in 1955, aged fifteen, I rode Mrs Wrathall's Penny Farthing all the way from Kentmere to Windermere. I was dressed as a Mad Hatter and our form master asked me to do a demonstration ride around the cricket field, which was then in the centre of the school grounds. The photo (top left) shows me on my return to Kentmere with my brother Gerard and Father inspecting the machine.

When I bought my own Penny Farthing from my friend Tom Potter at Kirkby Stephen, the main wheel of the bicycle was slightly larger in radius than my inside leg. As a consequence it was difficult to mount because my trousers were prone to catch on the seat! The photo (left) shows the radius of the wheel of my Penny Farthing in relation to the length of my leg.

In 1973 I offered to ride my Penny Farthing from Bowness Pier to Ambleside Pier at Waterhead for the Round Table's Community Service Appeal. The distance was five miles. That summer at weekends we sold a large number of tickets for people to guess the time it would take. I did demonstration runs around the Glebe carpark and the tennis courts in Bowness. The reaction from the public at bank holiday weekends was hilarious! The guesses ranged from 20 minutes to 17 hours! The Penny Farthing ride actually took 32 minutes and 8 seconds. I only had to get off once and walk up the hill near the famous Miller Howe Hotel. Then I rode the rest of the way at a gallop! I was timed cycling at 26 miles an hour on my ancient steed along the A591 down the hill from Troutbeck Bridge past White Cross Bay. Truly a Century Old Flyer!

# DEW BATH ON A MAY MORNING

An early May morning was breaking
Through mists in a dappled dawn sky
And shafts of golden sunlight
Cast rides through the meadows close by.

I seated alone on the terrace
Could hear from the garden ground
The rapture of Nature awakening
In the clear morning air all around.

The brush of the mighty Sun-God
On split-leaves of our large beech tree
Spot-lighted excited movements
On the palm of a branch near me.

Three little birds were dancing there
And bouncing playfully
Alert to all around them
Yet revelling merrily.

Then down to the dew-drenched lawn grass
They bathed in the morning dew
Beating their wings like a flurry of flails
While through the sunbeams droplets flew.

Never were diamonds more sparkling
Than those dewdrops in the sun
Never the heart more jocund
By such a joyful display of fun.

But in that glorious moment
While carefree in a world of their own
Came a helicopter–gunship magpie
Soundless and flying alone.

Attack can come without warning
In predation and Nature's law
Revulsion and hatred no solace
Mother Nature levels the score.

But like a bright flight of Red Arrows
They rocketed skywards asunder
Leaving one mesmerised magpie
And me? ...Well ... just lost in wonder!

LH May 1994. (Helme Lodge, Kendal)

Dew Bath on a May Morning.

# TO A WORLDLY LADY!

In the bath she is warm and caressing
She kisses and fondles your toes
Enveloping, embracing your being
In a way that only she knows.

In anger she's wild and exciting
Untamed, unbridled and free
A rainbow in double refraction
Or iridescent on the waves of the sea.

She appears in the soft glow of morning
Through curtains of gentle rain
In the form of a mermaid twinkling
Patterned on the window pane.

For she is the power, the Mother of Life itself
And Life is her only daughter
You may ask me who this phenomenon is:
I reply: *It is only Water!*

★    ★    ★

# LIFE ON TWO WHEELS WITH ROARING COMBUST!

There are things in life one should not miss
A first embrace and a tender kiss
The discovery of love, those nights of passion
When youth excels, no bounds, no ration!

Likewise when we lift the clutch and grip the throttle
Courage supplants fear; have we got the bottle?
The balance, the thrust, with the freedom to fly
All this we learn fast as the hedges shoot by!

The bumps, the scrapes of the learning curve
The going too fast; can we keep our nerve?
This maiden on wheels is so lithe and so lissom
To our wise inner voice we need to listen!

For all such sensation can lead to temptation
Though sometimes it feels good to give in
Nothing can compare to the fresh morning air
When over Shap we're out for a spin!

The ecstatic thrill as we crest Huck's Brow hill
With high velocity coming up on the dial
To a man growing old who won't be told
It gives rise to a satisfied smile!

My Yamaha was smoother by far than any car
Her brakes and the steering were fine
She was good for the thrills over Lakeland hills
And the ride: well, it was just divine!

And this is still so on my Moto Guzzi
For though I am older my head's not yet fuzzy
I can glide with my Jean, my wife, my soulmate
And feel like a young man fresh out on a date!

Revised 2011

LH on my old Sunbeam
on Banbury Run 2009

# FACES

The fact that there are millions of people on earth, all with different faces, is a continuing wonder and fascination for me. There are people who look similar and there are look-alike twins, but I fancy they make up a very small percentage.  A face is expressive and as variable as the weather; it seems to mirror the soul. How can all the faces on Earth be so different?

★   ★   ★

There are faces alike but still different
There are millions of faces on Earth
So how does the Great Creator
Make us all individual at birth?

Contrast cold clay of the death mask
Which sets as your loved ones depart
With the affectionate smile of the living
Sustained by a loving heart.

Yet most of our living faces
Are as changeable as the sky
One moment bathed in sunshine
The next: well, a cloud sails by!

On to this screen, this human canvas
Is projected from within
Maybe a soul open and honest
Or the stains of a hidden sin.

Contrast the fair face of pubescence
Innocent when in her prime
The blush, the rich embarrassment
When she attracts her mate first time.

No word or sound may be uttered
Yet the meaning between them is clear
The facial expression is more telling
And the warmth of exchange more sincere.

And so a new face is created
When the courting and nuptials are done
A new canvas conceived to be painted
Oh! The creation of faces is fun!

LH  5.04.1999

My 59th Birthday!

# A RETIRED SCOTTISH DOCTOR CALLS

Noo Doctor MacPhysic was retired you ken
And this was a story that was told to our Len.
The doctor returned to his own bailiwick
Where he had practised and cured most of the sick.

An avuncular man most caring and kind
A lovely old doctor, the best you could find
He called on two old ladies cultured and prim
Who were excited and delighted to welcome him in.

"Will you have a wee dram or a nice cup of tea?
Perhaps your favourite cakes like they used to be?"
So off to the kitchen the two ladies went
While he looked round and enjoyed the sweet flowers' scent.

The sun shone brightly across their boudoir grand
A beautiful Steinway with music on the stand.
But there in the sun's rays a small packet did glow
Curiosity got the better: he had to know!

A condom in a packet he was amazed to see!
What need had the ladies? How could this be?
So when the ladies returned with the tea on a tray
He enquired about the packet to see what they'd say.

"You see Doctor MacPhysic, we found it out on our walk
We read all that it said and we had a good talk;
'Place on the organ was the clear direction
To get full protection from any infection.'

Well Doctor, you see, we have no organ to play
So on our grand piano we placed it that day –

And do you know, Doctor, we haven't had a cold all winter!!!"

LH  2011

★　★　★

# A SPARROWHAWK'S DINNER

Like intermittent puffs of pipe smoke
Wisped away on summer breeze
So it is my eye is taken
By distant movement under orchard trees.

I lazy, lounging in the evening
Under Georgian façade
Where roses climb cast-iron veranda
A fountain plays in the old courtyard.

My evening slumber is soon discarded
Bird binoculars I take in hand
Sunbeams strike the floating feathers
As I focus on the orchard land.

A sparrow hawk has caught his dinner,
Alert and watching all the while
Plucking feathers from a ring-dove
His cold eyes scan radar-like, but never smile.

The hawk dissects the ring-dove swiftly
Mantles his prey with wings outspread
The dove's mate mourns across the orchard
Trembles and flutters in fear and dread.

★    ★    ★

Later I viewed his dining table
His plate a feather circle on the ground
No meat or skin was wasted
Only scraps of skull and claw I found.

Sad, yet nature breeds more ring-doves.
Of sparrow hawks we see but few.
When my time comes – come sparrow hawk
For I doubt if the ring-dove ever knew!

LH 5. 8. 1997

# HOMO SAPIENS?

Driving nature backwards
To the sterile wastes of hell
Men burn the earth still blindly
And destroy the living cell.

Do we think when we press onwards
How with ever mounting speed
We burn our life and energy
By materialistic greed?

More oil, more oil, we all proclaim
We must have more nuclear power
We build pipelines beneath the sea
And turn marine life sour.

In the name of economics
In pursuit of GNP
We lose the life we live for
If we don't stop and see

That nature needs a balance
And we our part must play
Lest animals, birds and flowers
We lose upon our way.

No grass to feed the cattle
No meat to eat or stew
No birds to eat the insects
And humans but a few.

LH 14.03.1974

# RENEWABLE ENERGY

## Reflections & regrets – some thoughts!

"Homo Sapiens" was written 37 years ago. I have always been interested in the generation of energy from water: hydropower and tidal power from the sea, as well as other natural sources of energy.

Apart from helping clients to pursue their projects in this area of work, I regret not having taken a more active role in promoting renewable energy long ago. Unlike Norway, the UK has not used sufficient of its revenues from North Sea gas and oil to build our own renewable energy resources.

Our past governments, it seems, have preferred to tie us to long-term agreements to bring oil and gas from the Middle East and elsewhere. We have spent a fortune on the infrastructure for doing so: funds which might have been better spent developing renewable energy capability and manufacturing here.

Fortunately, as oil prices rise and the countries producing oil have become unstable, we are at last becoming more focussed. We now have research and development going on at our universities and we have engineering skills in Kendal and at British Aerospace. Sadly most manufacturing of renewable energy systems at this time comes from Europe and abroad. Surely our skilled engineers, now being made redundant as war plane orders in this recession decrease, could turn their skills to making our own renewable energy equipment and plant?

Nevertheless there are exciting new developments for producing the energy we need and hopefully we will take a leading role. Wind turbines produce mixed responses from the public and clearly we don't want them all over the place. There are more interesting and reliable sources. Developments in solar power and ground source heating are producing good results.

Anaerobic digestion and biomass have a contribution to make, not only in energy production, but in reducing land-fill and turning waste into energy. Hydropower has been a source of energy for centuries but is underdeveloped. There is great scope for this in the Lake District, Scotland and Wales.

There is an experimental tidal-energy power plant on the island of Islay, not far from Portnahaven, which is unobtrusive. We have hundreds of islands and places around our shores where small tidal power producing units could be situated to feed the National Grid, but progress has been slow.

David Brockbank of Staveley has for some years been promoting his turbine and bridge proposal across Morecambe Bay to the Furness district. With turbines below the bridge activated by the tidal flow, it would not affect water levels in Morecambe Bay area or disturb the wildlife around the bay. A bridge across the bay would shorten the journey to and from Barrow-in-Furness and save fossil fuel.

If only we could develop our skills and our own manufacturing base to produce the turbines, we could develop opportunities to revitalise our home industries and provide apprenticeships and real work for our young people. For too long, investors have financed cheap manufacturing abroad for paper money. We have preferred to buy cheap goods from abroad rather than support our home industry and keep a balance. We are not short of ideas and great inventions, but our mind-set as a nation needs to change.

The farming industry is also experimenting in ways of covering energy costs and producing surplus energy for the National Grid, but will entrepreneurs and energy companies be allowed to get on with it? What will our planners say?

*Food Security*: There is an urgent need to develop an economical alternative to diesel oil in order to power farm tractors and food distribution wagons. We are now far too dependent on diesel oil to produce our food. Food security does not have sufficient attention. Oil is the fossil fuel which underpins the production of our food in the UK and also the importing of food by air and sea. We no longer have lots of small, self-sufficient farms with a large labour force to fall back on in a crisis, as was the case in the last war. Our navy is depleted and could not protect what is left of our merchant fleet. As most merchant shipping is now under foreign control in our global economy, our food supply from abroad is less secure.

It is also important that the districts of the U.K. support the production of food that is capable of being grown locally. By that means we can maintain the security of food supply locally. It may be economical now to produce monocrops of food elsewhere, but it leaves us exposed when food has to be transported, particularly if the oil supply is cut off or the price of oil rockets.

We must put more emphasis on the development of our manufacturing base in Lakeland. By doing so we shall be more secure and less exposed to the tidal flows of money when panic paralyses the markets and produces more and more pessimists. Such *Job's Comforters* undermine our confidence and promote what they predict. So let us banish the pessimists and get on with doing things. We need sustainable development and manufacturing appropriate to each community.

If we want good pensions on retirement we need to generate a greater proportion of the wealth required to do so from British industry and innovation. Our pension system in Britain was amongst the best in Europe until the main incentive to save in that way was removed. That in turn has affected the ability of retired consumers to invest and spend for the benefit of all. It is surely time to invest in a sound future for our children and grandchildren.

We have lived in "Cloud Cuckoo Land" too long. Our "candy floss" economy has melted. We can no longer afford to police the world except through the United Nations, properly financed by all the countries of the world, in proportion to their gross national output.

We are an inventive and innovative nation but so often our ideas are developed abroad through lack of national support and shortsighted monetarism. It is time for new thinking and for a new UK Industrial Revolution. We now know that university education alone does not fully equip young people for the world of work. We have undervalued the old apprentice system and the passing on of practical skills from experienced craftsmen and engineers; so now we are paying the price.

# THE DAWN CHORUS

It's a-funny spot is this auld world
But wat a grand spot t' be
When t' throstle sings his heart out
On top of t' auld yak tree
An t' blackie up on t' lectric powl
Sticks oot his chest an sings
Just t' fetch anudder day
As t' birds aw stritch ther wings

Ah wakened up just tuther mworn
Twas just aboot quarter t' fower
Ah gat mesel scraffeled oot o' bed
An stood at oor back dooer
Ah listened wid simple thankfulness
T' dawn chorus was in full song
An ah'l tell you this there's neea composer
Can match that merry throng

Ah stood thear in me neet clea's
Cos t' mworn was warm an still
An ah listened till aw oor feathered friends
Up on t' wooded hill
There was t' scoppie an t' warbler an t' pidgin
An t' craw an laal wee chitty wren
An cheeky sparra up on t' spoot
Was chitteren noo an agean

They were aw that thrang steaken their claem
Till a bit o' t' countryside
An ivvery bird, beath big an smaw
Was singen far an wide
Ah wunder why th'aw start t' sing
When t' darkness starts t' wane
It's nobbut for hawf an oor er seea
Than aw ga's quiet agean

Ah thowt t' mesel hoo lucky ah was
T' stan an listen thear
Cos some fwok travels far an wide
But nivver t' dawn chorus hear
Yer can keep yer sunny Majorca
An yer villa oot in Spain
Just give me aw them fedthered friends
An ther chorus agean an agean

Tommy Coulthard

# THE TASTE OF PICKLED DAMSONS

## *Evelyn Hayton's Recipe*

The taste of pickled damsons
It tingles round my tongue;
We had a pilgrimage to the Lyth Valley
Each Spring when I was young.
My Mother had been raised there
Where the blossoms bloom and blow,
The hedges and orchards team with fruit
To be preserved for the winter's snow.

The taste of pickled damsons
Mother's recipe I'll share:
Prick damsons first to fill your jar,
When you have time to spare;
Then half a pint of vinegar
With a pound of sugar boil,
And you'll be well rewarded by
This age-old country toil.

I love the smell of damson plums
When you pour the liquid on
And leave it standing in the bowl
Till twice twelve hours have gone;
Then pour the liquor off the plums
And bring it to the boil,
Mix and leave for one more day
Lest the delicious taste you spoil.

And oh the aroma of cinnamon!
Add two pinches to the pot;
Just a few cloves put in the mix
And boil again the lot;
Preserve your pickle in sealed jars
And wait six weeks for use;
Serve with your stews and casseroles
This delectable damson juice!

© LH 17.11.1998

## To a Phenomenon

You must be the most self – deprecating
Person who ever walked this earth.
You invite your friends to gather around you
And let them make you the butt of their mirth.
You take it all with extreme good humour
And beguile us with your delightful rhymes:
You never flinch from the bold confession
Nor falter in the difficult times.

How do you find the courage?
Is it the honey on the porridge?

You win the respect of all who know you
And the love of a charming and gracious wife.
Together you host a wonderful party
To mark a milestone in her life.
We celebrate with the greatest pleasure
Knowing there is real happiness there,
And both of you are the inspiration
For a JOYOUS evening that all can share.

What is the secret of the marriage?
Could it be honey on the porridge?

You wake at dawn in creative mood;
Joy wakes at six to prepare the food.
You steer your clients through the legal maze
Joy helps her Docs in so many ways
And still you have time for our highs and lows,
Our hopes and fears and our laughs and woes.

And so we unite to pay you homage……
And hurrah for the honey on the porridge.

*Elizabeth G.*

who also has honey on porridge

Written following Joy's birthday party on 18<sup>th</sup> January 2003

Picture of Elizabeth Gifford's poem

# THE BSE HOLOCAUST

I'm a cow
An innocent cow
Among thousands of cows like me.

I'm a docile cow
A friendly old cow
There are thousands of cows like me.

I'm a productive cow
A valuable cow
Milk flows from thousands of cows like me.

My ancestor cows
The war-time cows
Fed the nation from cows like me.

I'm a cow
An innocent cow
Condemned among thousands of cows like me.

★   ★   ★

I'm walking to death and destruction
To be burned and totally lost
There is meaning in life if they eat me
But now they waste all I cost.

Who are these humans to condemn me?
They rule by fear and by mob
Hysteria, a story, a sensation
Justice destroyed and truth they rob.

Where are the animal rights folk?
Do they stand guard at the furnace door?
Or are they silent in the mob
Like the holocaust gone before?

It's all may be, could be, rumour, might be
BSE is their fear and dread:
So innocent I go to slaughter
Sacrificed in a pagan ritual not yet dead.

I'm a cow ... an innocent cow ...

© LH May 1996

# GREEDY MAN
## *Should have a Rhumen like a Cow!*

Whativver did God mak Man fer?
Man wud be better designed as a coo.
I doot if we'd hev o these earthquakes
Ner 'oot o toon shoppen' we hev noo.

If we nobbut munched guss en wild floo-ers
Leav-en coo-claps ta nourish oor fields
We'd hev nay need fer plastic containers
En all t'rubbish that packaging yields.

North Sea gas we sowk oot fer heat-en
En pump billions o' gallons o' crude
Makken stinks as we burn hydrocarbons
Producen synthetic en tasteless food.

They say oor Earth spins roond en roond
With tsunamis and twisters, thur's summat amiss!
We've howked o'er much fuel fre out o' t'grund
Mappen we've knocked Earth off its axis!

If it's wark we mun spar oor muscles!
Modern hydraulics may do it instee-ad
With the time that we gain, we can jog oot in t'rain
Then do weight-lifting and strut-chen with lee-ad.

Nay wonder oor earth crust craks open
Nay wonder some hooses foe doon
Nay wonder oor climates garn crazy
En thur's Soddam en Gommorah in toon!

T'lile birds we've lost in gurt numbers
Their grub chain affected by greed
As man wid his global economy
Shops round t'world fer much cheaper feed.

So if Man was a bovine species
He'd nivver hev fed brains to a coo
So the BSE holocaust burning
Woddent be happenen noo.

Oh I wish we'd been designed with a rhumen
Ta munch guss en clover somehoo
We woddent need falderments ner transport
En GOLD en BANK CRASHES.
Well! … They mean nowt tull a coo!

*Postscript:*
*Since musing upon the aforesaid*
*My thesis has been stabbed through the heart!*
*Cows are charged with gross global warming*
*Allegedly from the METHANE they FART !!!!*

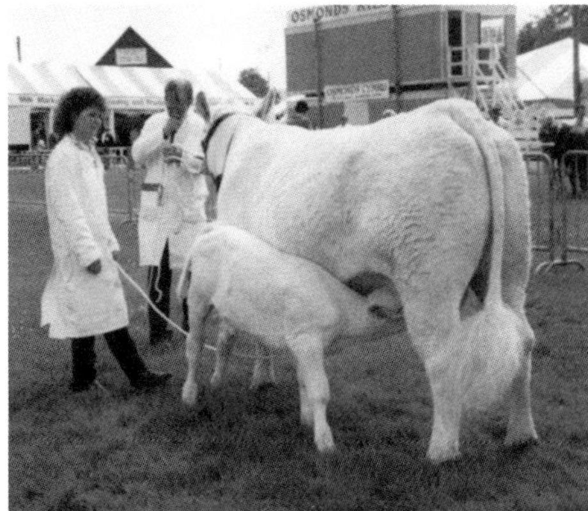

Judging of a Poll Charolais cow and calf

John Geldard, President Elect of the
Westmorland County Agricultural Show 2016

## SMILEY BUNGLE AND THE SLURRY TANK

Smiley en Bessie Bungle farmed in t'Lake District. Smiley en Bessie hed saved up en installed a new slurry tank. It was one o' them steel circle-types.

It was towards full en Smiley hed been up ta t'top of ladder ta tighten a bolt. While he was worken, he took his jacket off en hung it over t'top rim but it fell inta t'slurry.

Aboot 10 minutes later Bessie cem oot looking fer Smiley and he was naewhar ta be seen. Bessie hard some splutteren en swearen comen fre t'tank. So she climmed up t'ladder en looked o'er t'top o' rim. Smiley was swimming aboot in t'slurry.

"Whativver is ta dewen?" shooted Bessie.

Smiley cried, "I've lost mi jacket. It fell in and I mun find it."

"What!" shooted Bessie, "It will be nay good now."

But Smiley insisted, **"Nay, I mun find it! I will hev ta find it – mi sandwiches er in t'pocket!!!"**

# FOX versus LAMB

## (The Foxhunting Debate)

An early spring morning is breaking
Across the white waste of the sky
As sunbeams caress the fell tops
Lifting gossamer from pastures in-bye.

Twin lambs newborn are waking
And wobbling to their feet
Instinct urges colostrum
So they seek their mother's teat.

The ewe first licks their nostrils
So both her lambs can breathe
Consumes the membrane round them
Their new bodies to unsheathe.

A dog fox has been observing
From higher up the hill
Waiting deliberately waiting
To make advance and kill.

He has no need for breakfast
For his abdomen is full
Bloodletting is in his nature
And now he feels the pull.

There's no one here to help the ewe
She has neither fang nor claw
Her lambs are at their weakest
And the ewe can't bolt a door.

So she stands like brave Horatio
Stood on the bridge at Rome
Horns held high, she stamps her feet
To defend her heaf and home.

The fox moves round to mesmerise
Innocent noses nuzzle beneath
The ewe cluthers her progeny by her side
To protect them from its teeth.

By baiting the sheep till she charges the fox
The lambs are cast asunder
The fox now takes off with one of them
As she makes this timeless blunder.

The lamb's head now lies severed
With the body left to rot
Sometimes the head is buried
Is this a future fox delicacy? I know not.

★　　★　　★

I feel for the fox when hunted
Or when it is shot or maimed
I want to see beautiful foxes
But this killer will never be tamed.

The fox has no natural predator
Except in the form of Man
Thus the balance has been kept in a natural way
By hunting since time began.

Lamping with guns and poison
Snares, gassing, traps and pills
Are all abominable concepts
Far worse than the hunt and the spills.

The wisest and fittest fox from the hunt
Will normally escape away
To raise healthy cubs and maintain its line
Forever and a day

So leave us alone to our well-tried ways
Our country foxes are healthy and strong
If the fox was to vote, I conclude it would note
That the fanatics have all got it wrong.

LH 14.03.2006

# A BILLIONAIRE'S BANK LOAN

## (Rhyme based on a Mike Winkley story)

To a large Liverpool bank, a skyscraper in glass
Came a loan-seeking Ferrari owner, clearly upper class!
"Can you loan me five thousand, personal Bank Manager man
Take the Ferrari as security, if you can?

"I'll be back in three weeks the loan to repay
So calculate the interest up to three weeks today!"
The bank secured the Ferrari in its compound below
Did a credit check on the owner, but were puzzled to know:

*    *    *

An entrepreneur?
A famous billionaire?
Why a five thousand pound loan
When he has millions to spare?

*    *    *

When the owner returned from his foreign safari
Repaid his loan, his interest and collected his Ferrari
The Bank Manager bemused by his professional pomposity
Was determined to satisfy his puzzled curiosity.

"Why borrow £5,000: you've loads of money to spare?"
"Well, I placed my lovely Ferrari in your tender care.
You may think I'm a bounder, a spiv or a fool
But for thirty one quid
**It's the securest parking in Liverpool!"**

MSW/LH 2009

*    *    *

# GO WITH THE TIDE OF GOOD FORTUNE

### An Ode to a Cheerful Approach to Life

Be gone cold corpse of pessimism
Weak winter of weaker sun
Free the tide of good fortune
Which flows through your soul
And let your spirit run.

Open your face to the sunlight
Like a harbinger of spring
Let the tide of good fortune
Which flows through your soul
Make all your body sing.

Raise your eyes to the far horizon
Seek the beckoning pathway between
As the tide of good fortune
Which flows through your soul
Makes all of your journey serene.

Smile as you meet fellow travellers
For smiles are the sunshine of life
Then the tide of good fortune
Which flows through your soul
Helps others to free them from strife.

Rejoice in your Maker around you
Let good cheer range wide and free
For the tide of good fortune
Which flows through your soul
Raises awareness in all that you see.

Think on the mysteries within you
But don't ponder too long on the way
For the tide of good fortune
That flows through your soul
Flows on to another day!

LH  8.9.1998

# EPILOGUE

Recently out of the blue we received letters from Simon Boyle and Stephen Sykes who were trainee solicitors with Len at the Windermere office during 1988/1990. They now live in the south of England and while on holiday in the Lakes they came to visit us for the first time in August 2016.

Both Simon and Stephen have had illustrious careers in the field of environmental law and they set up a very successful environmental consultancy business together. They told us that they often spoke about Len and always held him in high esteem for the principles of law and practice which Len pursued in a very happy office atmosphere.

Simon still carried the Swiss Army penknife which Len gave him when he left Hayton Winkley and it has been his companion on many mountaineering and cycling adventures across Scotland and the Alps over the years.

Stephen, now Chairman of the UK Environmental Law Association, presented Len with following poem which he had written and which we both treasure.

# LH – THE LAKELAND LAD

What a piece of work this man:
How infinite his faculties: one who makes
His words sing and soar to his bidding,
Whose deeds resound like a mallet
Firm and resolutely –
Striking down the vale

When this man's hand defines a page
The words hit with the force of a waterfall
Cascading through the centuries of dialect:
Grandeur now: now laughter,
Then the epiphany of solace,
His wealth of wisdom to impart

This man lives not for the day alone:
All along the rugged bridleways of life
The seeds of memories he plants –
An enduring forest of oak and ash,
Hazel and the velvet-leaved beech,
Deep rooted here and ever strong of heart

★    ★    ★

Stephen Sykes, LL.B, MA
August 3rd 2016

# GLOSSARY

These are some notes on the influence of the Vikings on Lakeland place names and our dialect.

***Viking*** has become the common name used for the Norwegians and Danes who invaded our shores long ago. These Vikings could not all have been fierce warriors (pirates of the sea) but were settlers and farmers who intermarried with the local native population. The Vikings appear to have farmed on the higher ground in Lakeland and those who came from Norway must have felt very much at home among the Lakeland hills. They had a long-term effect on our dialect and family names and place names, as did the Angles and Celts who preceded them.

## HOO LANG IS "LANG SEN" IN LAKELAND?

*T'Anglians lant efta t'Romans went yam*
*En t'Norse com sean efta that*
*Noo I rayder like t'Scandinavian folk*
*Thur words en thur expressions en chat.*

*T'Normans nivver mannished ta tame us*
*Oor dales nut in t'Domesday Book*
*Oor forelders who valued thur freedom*
*Wud hev a fierce en formidable look.*

*In t'genes en blood of ald Lakeland folk*
*Thur's Celt en Anglian en Norse*
*The'v left thur mark on oor place-names*
*En in oor characters o' course.*

*Thur's "pen" fre t'Celts en "ton" is an Anglian yam*
*T'Norse browt "thwaite" en "beck" en "ghyll"*
*En if yan maanders aboot through Lakeland*
*Yan can see o sick-like origins still.*

$$\star \quad \star \quad \star$$

The Viking Era. It is generally accepted that the rise of Scandinavian influence on Britain began with the Viking raid on Portland Wessex in 789 AD and the raid on the Monastery at Lindisfarne in 793 AD. These raids were followed by raids on Iona in 795, 802, 806 and 807 AD. The Viking era of authority in England ended with the English King Harold's defeat of the Norwegian King Harald Hard Ruler and the routing of his army at the battle of Stamford Bridge in 1066. Viking influence in the Isle of Man and the Western Isles of Scotland continued into the 13th century.

Viking longship

We know the Vikings arrived on the River Liffey in Ireland with sixty ships in 837 AD and established the first Norse fortified settlements near Dublin in 841 AD. Evidence suggests that they settled, intermarried and were Christianised in Ireland but retained some of their pagan culture, before coming to Cumbria as refugees when they were expelled from Dublin in 902 AD. The Gosforth Cross in West Cumberland symbolises this, because it bears pagan as well as Christian symbols and carvings.

The Danish Vikings captured York in 867 AD and established themselves in Britain, mainly to the east of the Pennines with their stronghold in York, but with occasional incursions into the Eden Valley and around Penrith as DNA evidence confirms.

LH with the Gosforth Cross

In Kentmere in 1955, what is believed to be a Viking-type boat (carbon-dated *circa* 1300) was unearthed by Leslie Ridding when the Cape Asbestos Company was extracting diatomite from the old Kentmere lake bed. It is now in the Maritime Museum at Greenwich.

B. J. N. Edwards in his book, *Vikings in North West England – The Artefacts*, not only gives a comprehensive description and illustration of the spears found in Kentmere on Nan Bield Pass and in the tarn but also detailed information about burials, weapons, jewellery, coin hoards and sculptures found in Cumbria and the North West.

Then between 1981 and 1985, while I was still living in Kentmere, Steve Dickinson and his team discovered the remains of a Viking longhouse at Bryant's Gill in the Kentmere valley on the hillside beyond Hartrigg. The ten metre building with a central paved area produced a single radiocarbon date of the 8th or 9th century. The team unearthed eight lathe-turned spindle-whorls and twenty wet-stones together with iron artefacts, slag and worked stone believed to be from the Viking period. All these finds in Kentmere provide tangible evidence of a Viking presence in Lakeland.

Spindle whorls and whetstones from Bryants Gill, Kentmere, 8th or 9th century

# GENERAL BOOK GLOSSARY
## AS USED IN LAKELAND

Where known the origin of the word is shown by the following abbreviations:

**Celt** = Celtic
**D** = Danish
**Gael** = Gaelic
**Ice** = Icelandic
**N** = Norwegian
**ON** = Old Norse
**OE** = Old English
**WS** = West Saxon
**F** = Furness
**C** = Cumberland
**W** = Westmorland

**Aboon** = above
**Aboot** = about
**A crack** = a good talk or conversation
**Afoor** = before
**Ahin** or **ahint** = behind
**Alain** = alone
**Ald** = old
**Allus** = always
**Amang** = among
**Angry** = painful or inflamed (Ice)*angr*
**Anudder** = another
**Ark** = a chest, meal ark, the meal-chest (Ice) *örk*
**Arn** = own
**Aroond** = around
**Arval** = (adjective) anything connected with heirship or inheritance (Ice) *arfr*
**Arval bread** = cakes which each guest received at a funeral
**Atween** = between
**Aw** or **o** = all

**Ba-eth** or **beath** or **beeath** = both
**Baggin** = food or provisions
**Bairn** or **barn** = a child; anything born (Ice) *barn*
**Bane** = bone
**Barns** or **bairns** = children
**Bauk** = Beam to support the roof of a house (Ice) *balkr* a beam, naval bulk-head
**Be** or **bi** = by
**Be-ats** = boots
**Beck** = a river or stream
**Bedivilled** = bedevilled

**Begat** = begot
**Begattings** = generations
**Behint** = behind
**Belaa** = below
**Besom-stick** = birch stick
**Be-us** = beasts or cows
**Bid** = to invite, bespeak attendance (Ice) *bjóòa* – applied chiefly to marriage and funerals. The district within which all were invited to funerals was called a 'bidding'
**Bigg** = barley (Ice) *bygg*
**Bigum** = mild exclamation of surprise
**Biken** = biking
**Blacken** = to tell someone off
**Black Nanny** = the name for a kettle smoked black over the fire
**Blaa** = blow
**Blaaen** = blowing
**Blarn** = blown
**Blea** = lead coloured or blue (Ice) *blá*
**Blest** = blessed
**Bobby** = policeman
**Boggle(s)** = ghost(s) (ON and Celt)
**Boo** = bow
**Borra** = borrow
**Bow en scrape** = to pray
**Brant** = steep (ON) *brattr*
**Brass** = money
**Brat** = course apron – sackcloth (OE) *bratt*
**Breetly** = brightly
**Brig** = bridge
**Brossen** = bursting with food
**Browt** = brought
**Brutches** = breeches
**Bumly** = bumble bee
**Burra** = burrow
**Byre** = shippen, shuppen or cow house (OE) *byre*

**Cald** = cold
**Cam** or **cam steeans** = wall topping stone(s) (ON) *kambr*
**Canny** = nice or considerable
**Caps langcrown** = is beyond belief or very puzzling
**Causen** = causing
**Caw** = call

**Cem** or **com** = came
**Cem oot** = came out
**Chasser** = a chaser was a defective male sheep much given to pursuing and annoying females; a man with a similar propensity towards women was so named
**Chimley** = chimney
**Claggy** = sticky (D) *kloeg*
**Clapped** = clapped out thin
**Clarty** = muddy, sticky, unclean
**Clashy** = blustery or showery
**Clayuths** = clothes
**Clegg** = a cleg or horsefly (Ice) *kleggi*
**Clim** = climb
**Closet** = toilet (usually outside)
**Clowt** = clout
**Com** = come
**Commen** = coming
**Coo** = cow
**Coo band** = rope neck collar for tying up a cow
**Coo-claps** = firm dung of the cow
**Coppy steal** = three legged stool, milking stool (N) *kubbe stol*
**Coves** = calves
**Cowle** = to rake towards oneself
**Cowle-rake** = long-handled rake designed to pull manure from a horse-cart into heaps when spreading manure
**Craa** = crow
**Crack** or **good crack** = a chat, talk or good conversation
**Cragfast** = stuck on the ledge of a crag
**Crag Quarter** = North West Quarter of the Valley- See Index Ref. to Border Tenure & Kentmere Quarters.
**Craks** = cracks or fractures
**Cravacked** or **cravick't** = stiff-backed or stiff-jointed (WS)
**Creaked** = crooked
**Creel** = peat basket (ON) *krili*
**Cum** = come
**Cursmas** = Christmas
**Cush cush** = call to cows for milking (Ice) *kussa*

**Dadder** = to tremble or shake
**Dadderam shakkem** = jelly
**Dalt** or **dote** = a share in an open field
**Dee** = day
**Deead** = dead
**Deeaf** = deaf
**Deed** = died

**Deet** = to dress or make clean; hence: to winnow corn
**Deeter tray** = winnowing tray which shakes the grain from the husk within the thresher
**Deftly** = quietly, silently
**Der** = do
**Dess** = to pile up in layers (Ice)
**Deleet** = delight
**Donk** = to moisten or wet, as rain does; drizzly, applied to the weather
**Doo-er** = door
**Doon** or **dean** = down
**Doot** = doubt
**Dord-damn** = an epithet borne of upset or frustration
**Dote** = don't
**Dowly** = lonesome or dull (ON/Ice) *daligr*
**Dowter** = daughter
**Dross** = grossness, unwholesomeness
**Drush** = druf (Sc) fall to pieces or fall down
**Du** = do
**Dub** = a deep pool (ON/Ice) *djupr*
**Dunnet** = do not or don't
**Dyke** = ditch or water-course or drainage channel

**Easings** = eaves (Ice) *efesan*
**Eer** = year
**Efta** or **efter** = after (ON) *eftir*
**Elding** = fire or fuel (ON/Ice)
**'Em** = them
**En** = and
**Er** = are and or
**Eshes** = ash trees
**Esk** or **ex** = ask

**Fadder** = father
**Fa'** or **foe** = to fall
**Fain** = glad, anxious, fully disposed, joyful, willing (ON) *feginn*
**Fair** = quite, really, completely
**Falderment** = useless things, finery
**Fash!** = Bother!
**Fash** or **fashment** = to worry or bother
**Fasht** = weary or fed up
**Fassen** = fasten
**Feckless** = feeble and incompetent
**Feelens** = feelings
**Fell** = mountain (ON) *fjeld* (Ice) *fjall*
**Fella** = fellow
**Fend** = to provide or earn a living (Ice) *fe'na*

**Fer** = for
**Fergit** = forget
**Fer sham o thisel** = shame on you
**Fettle** = order, condition, to fit (Ice) *fella* (ON) *fitja*
**Feyten** = fighting
**Flacker** = flapping of wings
**Flayt** = frightened or nervous
**Flee** = fly
**Flit** = to remove from one house to another, as of household goods and chattels (Ice) *flytja*
**Flooers** = flowers
**Force** = a cascade or waterfall (Ice) *fors*
**Forrad** or **for'et** = forward
**Forelders** = ancestors, parents (Ice) *foreldri*
**Fowt** = fought
**Fratchen** = disputing and disagreeing
**Fre** = from
**Freet** = fright

**Gaa** = go
**Gaily weel** = very well
**Gallasses** = braces or suspenders
**Gang** = go or going
**Gang** = feeding passage or gangway between two rows of a skel-boose
**Garburn** = Garburn Pass from Kentmere to Troutbeck
**Garn** = going
**Garn a' bullin** = going with or taking a cow to the bull when it is on heat
**Garth** = an enclosure, generally used in compounds; a garden, also a small enclosed field close to the farmhouse (Ice) *garôr* (ON) *gardr*
**Gat** = got
**Gate** = a thoroughfare, a way (Ice) *gata*
**Gaum** = sense or forethought (Ice) *gaumr* heed or attention
**Gay** = rather, quite, somewhat
**Gay happy** = quite happy
**Geal** = to ache or tingle with cold, sudden pain
**Gavelock** or **geavlock** = steel crowbar
**Generally what** = usually
**Gill** or **ghyll** = small ravine, deep gully with stream (ON) *giel* (Ice) *gil*
**Gimmer** = female sheep under two years. Ewe lamb; a gimmer or ewe that has not lambed (Ice) *gymbr*
**Giss giss giss** = the call to young pigs (ON)
**Giss** or **griss** = a pig or swine (Ice) *gríss*

**Git** = get
**Gitten** = getting
**Gloo-ered** = looked around hard to see
**God-fearen** = God-fearing
**Gowk** = cuckoo (Ice) *gaukr*
**Graa** = grow
**Granbarns** = grandchildren
**Grave** = (verb) to dig or break up the soil (Ice) *grafa*
**Grave peats** = to dig peats
**Greans** = groans
**Greeap** or **greup** = channel where dung and urine is dropped by the cow in the shippen
**Green Quarter** = South East Quarter of the Valley
**Gripe** = dung or manure fork
**Gris** or **grise** = swine, young pigs (D)
**Growen** = growing
**Grunded** = grounded
**Gurnen** = pulling a face, grumbling, being miserable
**Gurt** = great, big
**Guss** = grass
**Gussins** = grassings or pastures

**Hansom** = handsome
**Hap up** = wrap up
**Happen** = perhaps
**Happenen** = happening
**Har'd** or **hard** = heard
**Harnted** = haunted
**Hasky** = a Lakeland dialect word meaning a sharp, frosty morning, clear and bright
**Haver** = oats (Ice) *hafrar*
**Hay bay or hubbyshoo** = a commotion, disturbance, uproar
**Hay moo** = haystack in the barn
**Heafed** or **hefted** = pasture on fell where sheep are born and return to (ON) *hefda*
**Heaten** = heating
**Hebben** = Heaven
**Hed** = had
**Heead** or **heed** = head
**Hes** = has
**Hest** = a horse (Ice) *hestr*
**Hetta** = have to
**Hev** = have
**Hev a good crack** = to have a good talk or gossip (OE)
**Hezzel** = hazel bush
**Hey** = high
**Hinder pap** = last teat

**Hippins** = baby's nappies
**Hisk** = gasp
**Hissel** = himself
**Hoaf** = half
**Hod** = hold
**Hodden** = holding
**Hollow-belly** = severe hunger
**Hoo** = how
**Hoo-al** = hole
**Howe** = small hill or knoll
**Howk** = to dig or scoop out
**Hubbub** = loud discourse
**Hubby-shoo** = a state of confusion; trouble or controversy; a commotion, affray or noisy gathering
**Hurpled** = lame, stiff, limping
**Hurplen** = limping, stiff with age

**If you would** = if you understand
**Insteead** = instead
**Intacks** = high pastures walled in from the fell
**Intul** = into
**I'se** = I'm, I am
**Ivver** = ever

**Jike** or **gike** = knock, creaking sound

**Keisty** = picky over food
**Kekt** or **Keckt** = tipped up
**Keld** = a well or spring (Ice) *kelda*
**Ken** = to know, be acquainted with (Ice) *kenna*
**Kent** = knew
**Kessen** = lying flat on back with legs in air – may be kicking or dead
**Ket** = dead meat, foul-smelling rubbish
**Kine** = cows
**Kirk** = church (Ice) *kirkja*
**Kissened** = burnt or overcooked
**Kist** = a chest (Ice) *kista*
**Kittle** = finely balanced, excitable
**Knaa** = know
**Knott** or **knot** = small, peaked hill
**Kytle** = a smock or loose jacket worn by farmers

**Laa** = low
**Laa groond** = low ground or bottom fields
**Laik or lake** = to play as children do, to amuse oneself (Ice) *leika*
**Laiked** = played
**Laiken** or **laiken aboot** = playing (ON) *leika*

**Lait** or **late** = to search for, to seek (ON) *leyta* (Ice) *leita*
**Lang** or **lang sen** = long or long ago
**Langer** = longer
**Langins** = longings
**Lant** = landed or arrived
**Lan't back** = landed back or came back
**Larn** = learn
**Larnin** = learning or study
**Larnt** = learned
**Lathe** = a barn (Ice) *hlaôa*
**Laylick** = lilac
**Leak** or **leuk** = look
**Leak efter** = to look after, care for
**Leaven** = leaving
**Lee** = a lie
**Leead** = lead
**Leet** = light
**Leeved** = lived
**Ligs** = lies
**Ligged** = lain or lay
**Liggen** = lying down
**Likesear** = likewise
**Lile** = little, small
**Lile lasses** = little girls
**Lish** = agile
**Loave!** = exclamation of surprise or delight
**Lonnin** = green lane, path or road, country lane (ON) *leyna*
**Lontered** = loitered or dawdled
**Loosed doon mi galasses** = unfastened my braces
**Louked** = hit or struck
**Loup** or **lowp** = jump
**Lowe** = flame, blaze
**Lownd** = calm, still, quiet (ON) *logn*
**Lowped** = jumped
**Lowse** and **lowse oot** = release harness or yoke (ON) *laus*
**Lowsen** = to loosen, untie
**Lug** = ear

**Maaen guss** = mowing grass
**Maanders** = meanders
**Maazled** = amazed or puzzled
**Mainly what** = usually or most times
**Maist** = most
**Maister** = master
**Makken** = making
**Macks** or **maks** = makes, kinds or sorts
**Mannish(ed)** = manage(d)
**Mappen** = perhaps, maybe
**Marpment** = daftness, silliness
**Marra** = friend

**Mair** or **mayer** or **mear** = more
**Mart** = market
**Mebbe** = maybe
**Meckins** = profits
**Med** = made
**Meedas** or **meeders** = meadows
**Mekken** = making
**Mendit** = mended
**Menny** = many
**Merry neet** = merry night: a social gathering of country people, usually involving a hot-pot supper, the drinking of good ale with volunteers singing, telling tales and reciting verses, the proceedings gently guided by a jovial MC
**Mi** = my
**Mickle** or **muckle** = large, much, great (Ice) *mikill*
**Midden** = heap of farmyard manure
**Milk be-us** = milk beasts or milk cows
**Milken side** = space between cow and rud-stake where there is room to sit to milk
**Moidered** = bothered or perplexed
**Mon't** = mustn't or must not
**Mooan** = moon
**Mowdy** or **mowdywarp** = mole
**Mudder** = mother
**Mun gang** = must go

**Naybody** = nobody
**Neb** = beak
**Nebbers** = neighbours
**Neet** = night
**Ner** = nor
**Neuk** = nook or corner
**Nicked in t'heed** = wrong in the head
**Nin** = none
**Nivver** = never
**Nobbut** = only
**Noo** = now
**Nowder** = neither
**Nowt** = nothing
**Nut** = not

**O** = all
**O'** = of
**O'er** = over
**Oor** = our
**Oot** = out
**Owt** = anything

**Pap** = teat
**Parlish** = remarkable, wonderful, noteworthy, extraordinary

**Physic** = medicine
**Piggin** = a wooden drinking cup (Gael) *pigeon* – not the bird!
**Pike** = hill-top (ON) *picke*
**Pill-dill** = a happy gathering
**Poapen** = walking in the dark
**Poddish** = porridge
**Pow** = wooden pole
**Prop't** = propped up
**Proven** or **proggin** = animal food
**Puddles** = (verb) muddles or confuses
**Pund** = pound

**Rannel boak** or **baulk** = large beam running across chimney nook (Ice)
**Rader** or **rayder** = rather
**Raken** = wandering, roving about
**Reddy** = ready
**Reean (F) rein** or **rane (C & W)** = head-rigg or unploughed area
**Red drench** = animal medicine or tonic
**Reek** = smoke (Ice) *reykr*
**Reet** = right
**Renart** = fox (F) *renard*
**Ridge** = ridge (ON) *rigg*
**Riggen** or **riggin** = ridge of a house
**Ring widdy** = a ring swivel ring to which the cow band was attached
**Rive** = to rent or tear asunder, to pull or tug violently (Ice) *rifa*
**Roards** = roads
**Roon** or **roond** = round
**Rough brat** = apron made from sackcloth
**Rowentree** = rowan tree or mountain ash (Ice/ON)
**Rud** = red
**Rud-stake** = post to which cows are tethered in a byre
**Runnen** = running

**Sae** or **seea** = so
**Saggen** = sagging or dropping
**Sammel** = gravel
**Sang** = song
**Sark** = a shirt (Ice) *serkr*
**Sarra** = to feed or serve animal stock
**Sarra t'coves** = feed or serve the calves
**Sarved** = served
**Sayem** = same
**Scale** = Scale Farm
**Scales** = hut or farm (Ice) *skali*
**Scrammelled** = scrambled
**Scrowe** = a state of disorder, untidiness or confusion
**Scrowe of barns** = a large number of children

**Se-an** = soon
**Se-an on** = early on
**Seanest** = soonest
**Seeves** = rushes (Ice) *sef*
**Segg** = a hard callous place on the hand or foot (Ice) *sigg*
**Sen** = since
**Settlestean** = bed where cow lies down
**Shadders** = shadows
**Shaken** or **shaken** = shaking
**Shuppen** or **shippen** or **shippon** = cow-house or byre (OE)
**Sham** = shame
**Sheep lots** = enclosed sheep fields
**Shipperd** = shepherd
**Shoppen** = shopping
**Sick** or **sec** = such
**Sid** = saw
**Sike** or **syke** = a small stream or gutter, a wet ditch or drain (Ice) *siki*
**Sile** = to strain milk
**Sindens** = last morsels
**Skel-boose** = cow stall for a pair of cows
**Skoggerslops** = untidy person
**Slaa** = slow
**Slape** = slippery (Ice) *sleipr*
**Sleck** = to quench, to extinguish (Ice)
**Smit** = sheep mark (Ice)
**Smithfield** = Smithfield Cattle Show and market in London
**Snaa** = snow
**Sneck** and **sneck possit** = door latch and latch wedged shut to suitor
**Sneck-lifter fee** = entry fee or loan fee
**Soart** = sort
**Somehoo** = somehow
**Soo-al** = soul
**Soond** = sound
**Sowk** = squeeze
**Sowked en eased ut ivvery pap** = squeezed and eased milk by hand from every teat
**Spane** = to wean lambs from their mothers
**Spar** = spare
**Sparra** = sparrow
**Spelk** = splint, a splinter or slip of wood (Ice) *spelkr*
**Springen** = sharp shooting pain in foot
**Stan** = stand
**Stang** = a post pole or shaft of a cart (Ice) *stöng*
**Stangin** = on evenings of Christmas Day and New Year's Day revellers would mount those they met astride a stang and carry them to a pub and compel them to stand drinks all round. Also note: **Riding t'stang** = when a man or woman of the village committed adultery they would be carried from house to house on a stang in disgrace (Ice)
**Starved** = frozen
**Stayvla-Gayt** = old name for Staveley
**Stee** = a ladder (Ice) *stigi*
**Steean** or **stean** or **stane** = stone
**Steg** = a gander (Ice)
**Stown** = stolen
**Streea** = straw
**Straw-walkers** = mechanism in the front of the thresher that throws the straw on to the ground
**Strutchen** = stretching
**Strutches** = stretches
**Sud** = should
**Summat** = something
**Sump** = mire, puddle, midden (D)
**Swardle(s)** = Swaledale sheep
**Sweltered** = overcome with heat (Ice)

**Ta** = to
**Taday** = today
**Tak** = to take
**Takken** = taking
**Tan** = two
**Taneet** = tonight
**Tarn** = small mountain lake (Ice)
**Taty-pot supper** = meat, potatoes, carrots, peas, black pudding, etc.
**Teamen** = teaming or overflowing
**Teck** or **tek** = take
**Teckins** = takings or receipts of money
**Tellen** = telling
**Telt** = told
**Than** = then
**Theer** or **thur** = there
**Thi** = thy
**Thisel** = thyself
**Thoo** = thou
**Thoosen** = thousand
**Thowt** = thought
**Thrang** = busy, working hard (ON/Ice)
**Throstle** = thrush
**Thur** = there or their or they're
**Thur's** = there is
**Toon** = town
**Thwaite** = a field or clearing; a piece of land cut off by a fence or enclosed; a fell or meadow (ON)

**Thyvel** = porridge stick, stirring stick (ON)
**Ticker** = heart
**Toon** = town
**Trantlements** = playthings, odds and ends
**Trunlins** = sheep droppings or muck
**Tul** or **tull** = until
**Turble** = very
**Turble grand folk** = very pleasant folk
**Turble laa watter** = downhearted, depressed, not very well or under the weather
**Turnip tops** = turnip leaves – they made a soft and fragrant mattress for early experiments in lovemaking!
**Twinter** = sheep over two winters old

**Udder** = other
**Ullet** = owl
**Ut** = at

**Varra** = very

**Wad** or **wud** = would
**Wain't** = won't
**Wake** = weak
**Wanten** = wanting
**War** = were
**Wark** = work
**Warnen** = warning
**War't** or **whar't** = where the
**Warse** = worse
**Wat** = what
**Watter** = water
**Wedder** = weather
**Weel** = well
**Wemly** or **wemmly** = wobbly or unbalanced
**Wha** = who
**Whar** or **war** = where
**Whativver** = whatever
**Whemmly** = tottering, unsteady
**Whenivver** = whenever
**Whick** or **wick** = alive
**Whisht** = quiet or silent; quietly or silently
**"White side oot"** = white lining out
**White-weshed** = white-washed in traditional Lakeland style
**Wi** or **wid** = with
**Widoot** = without
**Winda** = window
**Wo'** or **waa** = dry-stone field wall
**Woddent** = wouldn't

**Wo-en** = walling
**Woes** = walls
**Woo** = wool
**Worrits** = worries
**Wrang** = wrong

**Yaa** = an, one
**Yak** = oak
**Yak Bob Day** = 29th May when the sprig of an oak leaf is worn
**Yam** = home
**Yan** = one – See Shepherd's Tally
**Yan afoor** = before
**Yance** = once
**Yans** = ones
**Yansel** = oneself
**Yat** or **yeat** = a gate
**Yek** = oak (Ice) *eik*
**Yer** = your
**Yowe(s)** = ewe(s), female sheep

My father's Kentmere version of the Shepherd's Tally; see also Garnett's *Westmorland Agriculture* (1800-1900), page 166

| | |
|---|---|
| 1 Yan | 11 Yan-a-dick |
| 2 Tyan | 12 Tyan-a-dick |
| 3 Tethera | 13 Tether-a-dick |
| 4 Methera | 14 Mether-a-dick |
| 5 Pimp | 15 Bumfit |
| 6 Sethera | 16 Yan-a-bumfit |
| 7 Lethera | 17 Tyan-a-bumfit |
| 8 Hovera | 18 Tether-a-bumfit |
| 9 Dovera | 19 Mether-a-bumfit |
| 10 Dick | 20 Gigget or giggot |